How to Train your Political Animal

A power handbook for changing yourself and your world

Melinda Maddock

Published in Australia in 2022 by Melinda Maddock

Website: www.melindamaddock.com

Copyright © Melinda Maddock, 2022

Design, cover artwork and illustrations by Cathy McAuliffe

NATIONAL LIBRARY OF AUSTRALIA

A catalogue record for this book is available from the National Library of Australia

ISBN: 978-0-6452405-0-4 (paperback)

Melinda Maddock .com

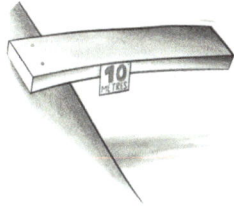

Contents

For David, Daisy and Harvey

Why are some people better at getting the outcomes they want?

It's not because they're smarter, or their ideas are more worthy.

It's because they're better at the politics.

You can be too.

It's time to train your political animal so you can do politics differently and create a better world.

About the author

Melinda Maddock marched to save Tasmania's Franklin River at the age of 10 and organised a national student petition for world peace at the age of 14. She shaped a career as a political adviser and senior bureaucrat, with extensive experience in social policy, climate change, strategy and campaigning. She is a speechwriter, and facilitator of changemaker workshops in her own consulting business where she helps people in organisations and communities use their power to make change.

Author's note

"

I have been gathering the words for this book since I started seeing the world as something outside of myself. I have read and collected articles and quotes by other people, observed and made notes of what I have seen and heard, and have learned from my own experiences. Over the years I have rewritten and reshaped the ideas of others – for public policy and articles, speeches and workshops. I have provided references where I can and appreciate any feedback on sources I may have missed.

I acknowledge the people who would have no idea of the impact they've had on my thinking and practice over the years. I have protected the identity of those who shared their stories with me in interviews and workshops by changing their names. I have also changed some details about the context of their stories to make sure I don't give their game away.

"

Introduction

In April 1986 the United States bombed Libya. I was watching the television news on the other side of the world in my brick-and-tile home on the peaceful island of Tasmania, at the edge of the Southern Ocean. I was 14 years old and I was outraged. It was the International Year of Peace – what did the adults think they were doing to my world? My teenage anxiety was already high, being consumed as I was by the tensions between the US and USSR, and the threat of it all going nuclear. I remember my mother was ironing at the time. She stopped, put the iron firmly up on its end and asked me, 'Well what are you going to do about it?'

That was it. All the permission I needed. I went to school with an idea to ask all Tasmanian school students to sign a petition for world peace and an end to the arms race. With the help of a Tasmanian Senator, the idea grew into a nation-wide petition that ultimately contained the signatures of 75,000 Australian students. We presented it to the Prime Minister on the steps of Parliament House in Canberra later that year. At the time, in the days before the internet, we were told it was the single largest petition to be tabled in the House of Representatives on a single day. And of course we achieved world peace. Well we didn't actually – you may have noticed. But that's not the point of the story. The point is a 14-year-old girl learned through that experience that she had the power to make change. Never again was power a negative word; it was something we all had a bit of. What we used it for was up to us.

I shaped a career as a political adviser and senior government official, always wanting to change the world, to question the way things were done and to do things differently. From working up close with leaders and decision-makers I saw the injustice in the way power was distributed. Those with the passion and will to change their community sat at the margins of society; they were largely invisible to the decision-makers, their voices unheard. Those at the centre held the power but lacked the will to use it to make change for good. Doing what was right often fell down the list, behind risk and reputation.

In more recent years as a consultant I have run workshops that help participants see and use their power to make change. It is always fascinating to hear people's responses to that word, *power*. It brings up associations like: big corporations, abuse of, privilege, big noting, money and elitism. It also generates words like passion, knowledge, confidence, leadership, strength, energy and change. I have learned that how people perceive power depends on their life experience, and that it's important not to make assumptions about that. If someone lives in a low-socioeconomic-status suburb they can still feel powerful in their own life. Just because a person is a CEO doesn't mean they have an entirely positive view of power either.

To be quietly powerful is to gently question, to nudge and encourage, to drop ideas into the ears of the decision-makers, and to bring the right people together to make things happen.

Being an introvert with a fear of conflict operating in the noisy, adversarial world of politics, I had to craft my own version of power. It's a quiet power. Behind the scenes I shaped public policy for others to announce and wrote speeches for others to deliver. In many ways it's not very brave to let others be out front. In other ways I got a lot more done by quietly walking the corridors, listening and observing, pulling the pieces together into something that made sense. I felt very powerful. I didn't ever need the accolades; all I needed was that something changed and someone's life was better as a result. To be quietly powerful is to gently question, to nudge and encourage, to drop ideas into the ears of the decision-makers, and to bring the right people together to make things happen.

Yet all around me I would see the symptoms of powerlessness. It showed up in words and tone, in sarcasm, cynicism and frustration. The passionate people would get worn down and then give up because it was just too hard to get change. They had tried and failed too many times and it was easier in the end to just go with the flow. These are the people who had lost the spark from their eyes and ended up just turning up. But their hearts were still good. What they needed were a few tools to help them do the politics.

We live in a crazy world with big problems that need solutions. Every day we put up with little problems that drive us nuts. We work in organisations and interact with systems that have forgotten we're human. We have under-valued and under-resourced service organisations that are trying to help rising numbers of people experiencing depression, isolation, addiction, homelessness and poverty. On top of that are the global challenges of displaced people, inequality, climate change and biodiversity loss. And now a global pandemic that has sent the world into free fall.

I look out at these enormous challenges and I feel like the potential to solve them is all locked up inside the people who've been worn down. The power to make change is there, but people think they don't have any power, or they don't know how to use it. It's like a light trapped inside a shell – you wouldn't even know it was there. So I see this book as a little hammer, which I'm hoping you can take and use to gently tap at your shell to make cracks, to break it open and let the light out.

It's time. **For those of us who have worked behind the scenes to get change, it's time to be visible. For those who are tired of trying, it's time to get a different perspective. For those who have chosen a comfortable life, it's time to get uncomfortable. For those who are afraid, it's time to ask for help. It's time to imagine a world where every 14-year-old has the opportunity to step into their own power. This book is the product of 30 years of quietly observing and participating in a political life, and I hand it over now for a new generation of political animals to take up.**

Politics is not a dirty word

These days politics has a pretty bad rap, but it didn't start out being such a dirty word. It comes from the Greek *politikos*, meaning that it relates to the *polis* or city-state, which back in ancient Greece was a community of several villages. When Aristotle, the so-called father of political science, wrote the line, 'Man is by nature a political animal', he was talking about the social instinct of human beings. He believed that when individuals are isolated they are not 'self-sufficing', and that people need to form partnerships and cooperate with others in order to achieve a common goal.

In Aristotle's *polis*, communities are self-sufficient and are not only able to survive, but to live well. So communities may come into existence to meet basic human needs, but they continue 'for the sake of a good life'. The *polis* is a political partnership: a collection of human beings who are able to live together by creating laws that allow for the survival of the community and the flourishing of individuals. Just like First Nations peoples did for many, many generations in their nations that came to be called Australia.

For Aristotle, politics was a practical science that was all about noble action, the happiness of citizens and serving the human good. Politics is a social activity; it's not something you do alone. So when you imagine that literary loner, Robinson Crusoe, on his island working out how much food he could eat every day, he wasn't doing politics. But as soon as Friday appeared and Crusoe had to make sure there was enough food for both of them, it was political. In allocating scarce resources there was a political relationship between them. While they cooperated in order to survive and flourish, Crusoe made sure that he was the master and Friday was his servant.

Somewhere along the path of history the meaning of politics changed. Ask people today what politics means to them and they come up with words like corruption, self-interest, ego, game players, control, greed and fear. They certainly don't see politics as something *they* do, but as something done elsewhere, and done *to* them. These views are similar to those of Samuel Johnson in the 1700s, who said that politics was 'nothing more than a means of rising in the world'.

How to Train Your Political Animal embraces the idea that politics is part of being human, being a social animal. In this sense it's closely aligned to the 20th-century political theorist Hannah Arendt, who talked about 'authentic politics' as 'different people getting along with each other in the full force of their power'. When we come together to act collectively for a good life, we are expressing our individual differences and using our power. This is a political act.

When we act collectively to care for people who are strangers to us, we are acting politically.

Decisions are made every day that are shaped by politics. Think about the responses to COVID-19. In all their human diversity, politicians, scientists, manufacturers and medical professionals have come together on a global scale to work out how to coordinate and direct resources to serve the common good. When we act collectively to care for people who are strangers to us, we are acting politically. For the political animals embarking on the training in this book, politics is a practical activity that is defined as: *Using your power to get an outcome that benefits someone else.*

The gift of a blank slate

In workshops when I am helping people imagine a different future, I ask this question: 'If you weren't already doing it this way, how would you do it?' The question leads us into the land of blue sky thinking. We get out our felt tip pens and draw multi-cultured utopias on butcher's paper. It's a fun activity, but somehow the grey cloud of reality-check always creeps in. People are realists. They can easily see the things that get in the way of their imagined future, like the pessimistic boss, the onerous processes, the lack of time and money. We always seem to have to bolt solutions onto systems that already exist, systems that have grown organically, like the hand-built hut layered up with bits from the tip shop. We never get the chance to imagine a better future from the place of a blank slate. That is until 2020: *Tabula rasa*, our blank slate.

I don't think I'm exaggerating when I say that humanity is in an extraordinary period of transformation. Disruption was a thing even before the global pandemic hit, and now change is on double time. Everything we thought was set in stone is now up for grabs. The tectonic plates of our old systems – our health system, education, democracy, capitalism – are all shifting beneath our feet.

Now we have a once-in-a-generation gift to create a world utterly different to what it has been.

We are reinventing the way we work, the way we learn, how we spend our time, how we relate to each other and how we live sustainably on the planet. The conversations about change that we had before we closed our doors to keep out COVID-19 feel as though they were hypothetical. Now we have a once-in-a-generation gift to create a world utterly different to what it has been. It's going to be a bumpy ride for a while yet, but that doesn't mean a permanent state of *Mad Max* is just around the corner. What it's going to take is for more people to use their power for good wherever they are – in families, at work, in their communities.

The green shoots of change are already there – we are all having to do things differently. Will we keep having compassionate conversations with our colleagues now that we've seen inside their homes online, met their pets and been with them at their most vulnerable? Will we get together with our neighbours to improve our communities now that we've swapped fruit and vegetables on our doorsteps? Will we still create meaningful connections with our customers now that they're no longer walking through our doors? It is going to take some work to make sure we don't snap back to business as usual. Our mode of politics is starting to feel like that swanky Size 8 suit we've held onto since our 20s: it just won't fit anymore. But rather than tossing it out holus-bolus, let's upcycle that old suit called politics and see what happens.

You're not stuck in traffic

So in all this craziness are you that person stuck in traffic, alone in your car, frustrated and angry that you're not moving anywhere, all these people in your way? It's hell out there. The goddamn traffic! Oh no, wait, dark cloud of revelation forming overhead, raining down little messages onto your bonnet like a scene from *Stranger Things*. An ominous voice booms through the roof, 'You're not stuck in traffic; you *are* the traffic!'

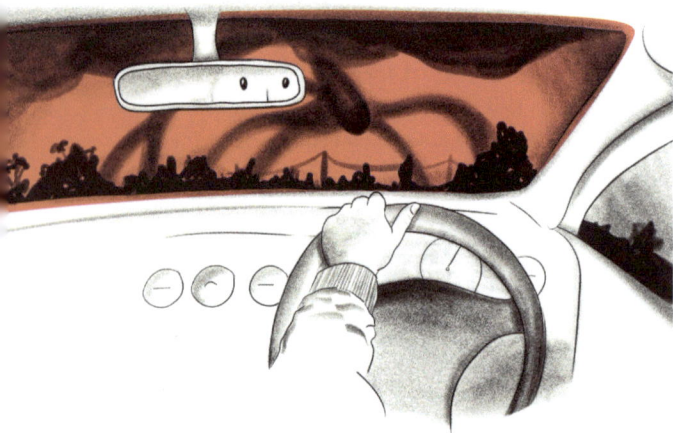

It's the same with systems: the transport system, the tax system, the economy, education, government. It's all so big and overwhelming and complicated and broken. 'They should fix it.' Hang on, who's *they*? *You* are they. You're not stuck *in* the system; you *are* the system.

While the system may feel enormous and you may feel minuscule within in, it is really just a construct made up of many tiny parts. The tiny parts are made up of many, many decisions made by individual human beings. Some of these decisions were made with good intentions and a sound evidence base. Some were made in a rush to tick a box and get it off a desk, even after a person like you put up a valid protest. And some were made out of self-interest, while a person like you stood by, knowing it was wrong but not knowing how to stop it.

> *Every doorway is an opportunity for you to shove your foot in and show a better way.*

Now think of each of these decisions we make as like little doors from *Alice in Wonderland*. They open to many other possibilities for making a better decision. Every doorway is an opportunity for you to shove your foot in and show a better way.

How to use this book

There's plenty written on the evils of politics: the power games, the psychopaths in the workplace and how to deal with them. This book is not about that. *How to Train Your Political Animal* is a practical guide for people who know that there's politics going on around them, but they can't understand it and don't know what to do about it. They know someone is playing power games, but they can't see their own power to change the situation. Quite frankly, some people are just good at politics; they are born with innate strategic talents. They have a clear sense of what outcome they want. They know what tactics are available to them and they are able to make a judgment in the moment about which one to choose.

If politics does not come naturally to you, the good news is that you can learn.

If politics does not come naturally to you, the good news is that you can learn. The advice to new players from the instinctive political animals I talked to for this book is to work out what your end game is, stay focused on who you are there for, and be disciplined in writing down your plan. Whether you're in a business, part of an organisation, on a committee, or in a community you love, as a worker, consumer and citizen you are invited into this call to action.

This book is both a training guide and a manifesto for a new way of doing things. It will help you use your power to do politics better, so we can all benefit from better decisions and a better world. It will teach you the lessons from the 'old political animals' that we're more familiar with, where self-interest and transactional relationships prevail. And it will show you the steps on the path to becoming a 'new political animal', whose self-awareness and meaningful relationships are the norm. You'll learn that the path from old to new is certainly not linear: there is plenty we can take from the old as we shape the new.

How to Train Your Political Animal acknowledges that politics isn't just something that happens in parliaments and boardrooms. So it includes real stories from everyday people – not the traditional experts, political scientists or MPs – but people like you and me who experience politics in their own lives.

The book takes you on a journey from the inside out. It starts by focusing attention on the world around you and within yourself in Chapters 1, 2 and 3. This is about using your personal power. It then expands that attention into your relationships in Chapters 4 and 5, with a focus on groups and teams in Chapter 6 (your relational and collective power). Across the chapters your 'power within' will transform into your 'power with'. The lessons learned are brought together in the final chapter, as you set out as a political animal to do good in your world.

Each chapter of the book includes 'practice tips' with questions that help you develop new habits every day. You won't just read this book and magically transform into the powerful human you always wanted to be. Becoming a political animal requires a change in mindset, so the tips help you self-reflect and try new behaviours.

You can no longer stand by – you need to jump in.

We are training your political animal for a politics that is being reinvented through every decision and every action. You might be relieved to know that you don't need to change the whole world, certainly not by yourself. What you can do is change *your* world. To make it happen requires you to first step into your power, embrace your political animal and start making better decisions. You can no longer stand by – you need to jump in. Your workplace needs you. Your community needs you. Your country needs you. Our planet needs you. It's time to do politics differently, everywhere, every day.

Chapter 1: Jump in

One of the penalties for refusing to participate in politics is you end up being governed by your inferiors.

– PLATO

There was once a good person called Heidi. She was pretty happy when she landed her first government job not long after finishing her degree in public administration. With all the energy of a bright, well-read 20-something she bounded into her new workplace full of ideas and dreams. Looking around the corporate division of this government agency with fresh eyes, she quickly spotted some practices that needed to be tossed into the 20th-century dustbin.

She took it upon herself to kick off some changes by redesigning the organisation's performance management processes. The latest research she'd read said that regular team-based performance management gets better results than the dreaded annual individual performance review. So she started drafting a paper for the executive team. Of course they'd love it – wasn't it the perfect antidote for a work environment that had poor productivity and was low on trust? Who wouldn't want to cultivate healthier relationships?

While Heidi was able to see some things pretty clearly as a new employee, there were some important clues she missed. She'd arrived in a workplace where people dipped their heads below the partition and quietly got on with what they needed to do. The unspoken rule was, 'If it ain't broke don't fix it in case someone notices that you still exist and wants to make an efficiency dividend out of you'.

Heidi worked for weeks on her paper, pulling in evidence from other jurisdictions and designing a model for implementation in her organisation. When she was happy with it she took it to a meeting of her managers and presented it with her characteristic gusto under 'Other business'. You're probably not surprised to learn that she didn't get the response she was hoping for.

Afterwards she described it as like poking a sea anemone with a stick and watching it shrink back into itself. With pursed lips, the senior manager politely nodded and pointed out that while they encourage different perspectives, Heidi hadn't followed the correct process. After the meeting Heidi's own manager took her aside and passed on some 'concerns'. She'd gone outside her position description and had lost focus on the original task, but that's okay – she's new and will learn. She was told to go back and update the individual performance management template to include a ratings matrix.

Heidi sat in her pod fighting back tears, wondering what the hell happened. Her bright flame started to dim. She looked out across the open space and contemplated how long it would be before she became like the others – just grateful that she had a job.

When we engage in politics we have a better chance of making good decisions and getting good outcomes.

Heidi's story is not uncommon. You probably recognise it; maybe you've even experienced it yourself. You start out with ideas and energy; you might dip your toe in the water and challenge some orthodoxies. Then you find you've been sidelined or labelled as difficult – you don't 'fit in'. So you challenge less – it's easier to go with the flow. Motivation drops and productivity declines and you find yourself just turning up. And the tragedy – for your organisation, for society and for the planet – is that the poor decisions happen when you don't participate. When we engage in politics we have a better chance of making good decisions and getting good outcomes. **It's time to jump in.**

Your power to make change

The most common way people give up their power is by thinking they don't have any.

Power is invisible when you have it and really obvious when you don't. In that way it's like a gas: you can't see it and when you don't know it's turned on it can kill you. If you live in any western country you are more likely to be aware of power and powerlessness if you are not wealthy, not white, and not male. Power isn't like oxygen: we don't all have enough to help us breathe and live. It is unevenly distributed in all of our systems: our democracy, economy, education, health and legal systems are made up of people who have more power than others.

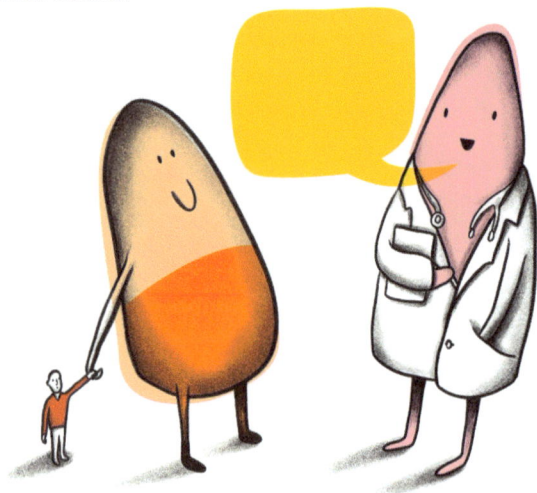

Children have an innate sense of their own power and powerlessness – they know they're smaller than everyone else, they're not as strong, and they don't know as much. That's why they sometimes have meltdowns in supermarkets. People who are skilled at working with children, like paediatricians, are very aware of the power differential. Watch a child's face light up when the doctor welcomes them into the room, looks them in the eye and asks, 'And who have you brought with you today?' – referring to the less important parents who've tagged along.

In a small regional hospital a physiotherapist called Tomas took a different view of power. He was working inside a hierarchical health organisation with dedicated health professionals who were stuck in old ways of doing things, inside a system that rarely stopped for breath. What Tomas noticed was that the doctors didn't always listen and the nurses could be judgmental. They always seemed to be busy – under pressure to meet increasing demands and in a rush to check the forms and get their tasks done. Tomas set out to change the way that health professionals relate to their patients. He decided to take a coaching approach to conversations with his patients, asking questions aimed at empowering them through their care. By doing so Tomas was consciously shifting the decision-making power from himself, the highly educated specialist, to the patient, the expert in their own body.

Everyone's experience of power is different. The purpose of this book is to first show you that you have some personal power and then to help you use it. The global pandemic has shown us that change can happen at a pace that we could barely imagine. That big systemic change is not taking place without us; it is happening every day in small ways, in every conversation, in every choice and decision. When we step into our power – when we share ours with people who are yet to find theirs – we create the change we want to see in the world. That is powerful.

It's all political

The former Premier of Victoria, the late Joan Kirner, was a highly respected and much loved mentor to women in politics. In her book written with Moira Rayner, *The Women's Power Handbook*, she explains why we ignore the machinations of politics at our peril: 'Every human transaction – family relationships, work, partnerships, contracts – is political, involves the distribution of power. If you don't claim your own individual power, someone may take it and use it, maybe against you. Those who do not act give away their power. Not to be interested in politics is as political an act as to insist on your share of power.'

In many places it's the person with the most power who wins, and they have the most power because they do the politics.

As a new employee coming in with fresh eyes, Heidi had a pretty good view of the organisation. What she didn't see, because it was well hidden, was the politics. She assumed a good idea would stand or fall on its merits. In some places that does happen, but in many places it's the person with the most power who wins, and they have the most power because they do the politics.

No one in the management team stood up for Heidi's initiative and idealism, or for the different approach she was proposing. They made a decision in that moment to maintain the status quo and therefore reinforced a culture that rewards conformity. Heidi did not use her power to make change and neither did the managers. So the senior manager won. And so did the poor decision to continue with annual performance reviews.

The consequences of poor decisions are quite serious. In Heidi's organisation there are teams of people putting hours of work, costing many thousands of taxpayer dollars, into things that do not work and do not make a difference. Think of the decisions in your world. It's not just the big ones like axing an emissions reduction scheme in the middle of a climate crisis, it's the small decisions too. Like the badly designed form that asks for your address three times, or the new footpath that's too narrow for a pram. Remember that time a supermarket chain tried to sell peeled bananas wrapped in plastic?

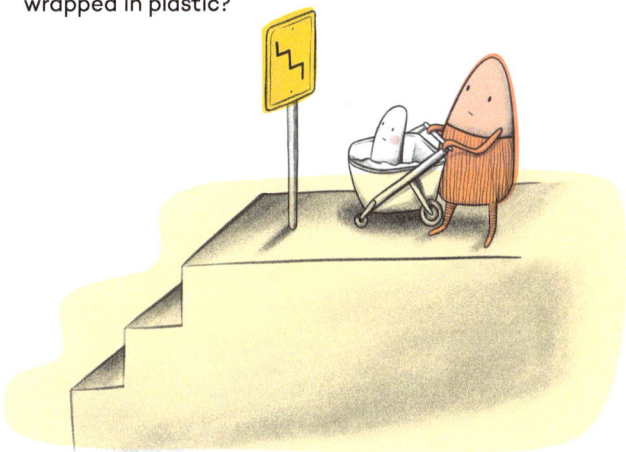

Human beings make decisions to do those things. Someone puts an idea forward and someone else says, 'Yeah, let's do it'. And then all this effort goes into making that thing a reality. Many excruciating hours of human effort making endless plans, in endless meetings about the endless plans, drafting endless revisions. What happens to the voices that ask, 'Do we really need to do this? Could we try this a different way?' In all likelihood that person is there somewhere. They may be lurking outside the door waiting to be invited in. They may be quietly blending in with the fabric on the sofa, worn threadbare after years of trying to make change. They may be banished to the basement with the other barefaced recalcitrants who dared to challenge accepted truths.

Maybe that person is you. I'm guessing that because you've picked up this book you're one of those genuine people trying to make sure the decisions being made are the right ones. But maybe you're not cutting through. Your views aren't being heard and your ideas aren't being taken up. You're over it, this feeling of pedalling hard and getting nowhere, watching people soaring past you tossing their crap decisions to the breeze and grinning as they land. Something's got to give, not just because you're feeling rubbish, but because we've got to stop the poor decisions, all of us together. We have a responsibility to make sure the decisions we are part of are better – much better – for the people and the planet, for today and for the generations that are coming behind us.

You need to play the game
to change the game

In the early days of her new role as CEO of a not-for-profit organisation, Nadia was learning how to navigate the complex web of government and political relationships. She was hesitant about it all, saying, 'I'm inclined to stay under the radar and not enter the fray'. She was scared of having to tiptoe through some sort of Machiavellian dystopia and step over corpses with knives in their backs. Fair enough. There are a lot of people with a vested interest in keeping things the same and they don't play nice. They have invested time cultivating their own power and they're pretty happy up there on their perch. They can be self-serving and power hungry. They may see you as a threat to their world view. It is safer to stay indoors and close the curtains. But when you do, nothing changes. If you want to change how it all works, this game of politics, then first you need to play the game.

It's not just Nadia – the very idea of politics for most people conjures up images of malevolent poker faces waiting around dark corners to do dastardly deeds. It's a nasty game, its players found lingering with evil intent around the office, at the board table, at community association meetings, in the playground, and of course in the corridors of parliament. Even the people who play it most overtly, the politicians themselves, denigrate their own profession, 'You're just playing politics', they say. How many other workers put down their profession in the same way? You don't hear the guys at the garage having a go at each other under the bonnet, 'You're just playing mechanics, mate'.

When more of the good people play the game, they will change the way the game is played.

So what if politics was different? What if it was less 'dog eat dog' and more 'dog share my food with you so we're all better off dog'? Or something like that. To reclaim the ground of politics for the common good, you and all the other Heidis are going to have to jump in and play the game. This is not good news for those who stand proudly at their morally high standing desk and proclaim to whoever is listening, 'I don't do office politics. *You hear me?* I. Do. Not. Do. Office. Politics.'

I get that they're not prepared to engage in this most brutish of workplace sports to advance their own career. But by not engaging, they are taking themselves out of important conversations that could make a difference. If good people like you don't play the game, then poor decisions are made. And the stuff that gets done protects someone's self-interest rather than the greater good. If you don't use your power, someone else will, and their motivation may not be as noble as yours.

When more of the good people play the game, they will change the way the game is played. This is what happened for Nadia. When she did 'enter the fray' she found regular human beings with challenges just like her own. She went on to foster meaningful relationships with her government funders, adapting her requests to meet their needs as well as those of her organisation, and they came to value her sector in a new way.

So imagine if our graduate Heidi had had a more aware manager. Someone who embraced her enthusiasm and nurtured her potential. Someone who could help her see her own power to make change and guided her with strategies to get positive results. Imagine a manager who was prepared to tackle the entrenched power dynamics in the organisation so that more people like Heidi could thrive. Heidi worked it out eventually. Through trial and error she learned what to look for in a workplace. She, and Nadia, are now part of a new generation of decision-makers who are participating and cooperating to make a difference for the common good. They are the new political animals and they're changing the rules of the game.

New political animals

In one sense the idea of participating in a political life is ancient. Indigenous people organised themselves and managed their resources sustainably for tens of thousands of years. It's also what Aristotle was going on about back in the 300s BC. But in his day the citizens who had rights and freedoms were limited; they certainly didn't include women or slaves.

Now we have the technology for mass participation, and younger generations coming through who are demanding to be directly involved in the decisions that affect their lives. There is tension in the way we organise between a triangle-shaped hierarchy with the expert at the pinnacle, and the flatter model of circles of interconnecting networks. The way power moves through these approaches looks fundamentally different. In their excellent book, *New Power*, Jeremy

Heimans and Henry Timms describe the differences between old and new power: 'Old power works like a currency. It is held by few ... New power operates differently, like a current. It is made by many ... The goal with new power is not to hoard it but to channel it.'

It's not only the use of power that's different; there are a few other features that set the old and new political animals apart. The first is how they see themselves: while old political animals are motivated by self-interest, new political animals are more reflective and self-aware. In relationships old political animals engage more in the transactional, coming from the point of 'I know best' and telling rather than listening. New political animals pursue meaningful relationships, honing their listening skills with the premise 'They know best'. In teams you may find that old political animals are more focused on their own power in the group while new

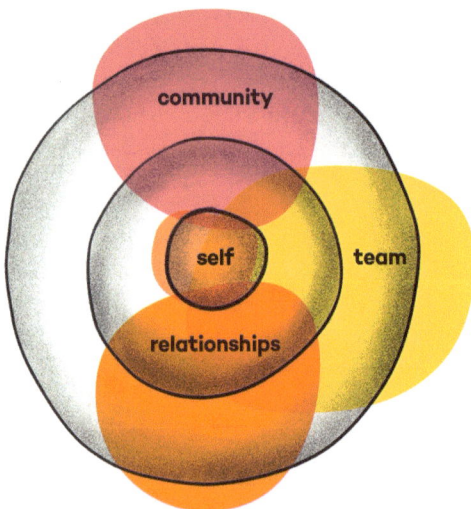

political animals seek power for the whole group and for others. In the broader community and society old political animals may see only one part and tend to look to the past for answers. New political animals see the whole system and are open to what the future brings.

To understand how the old politics works in practice, it's useful to have a look at the world of big P (party) politics. Power in political parties is organised into groups and sub-groups, also known as factions and voting blocs. Individual candidates are preselected through deals that are done between these groups, not through a merit-based selection process. Loyalty to these groups is generally more highly valued than skills, emotional intelligence and leadership capacity.

Political parties tend to attract and advance individuals who are more focused on their power in the organisation rather than the capacity of their organisation to empower others and make change.

Political parties tend to attract and advance individuals who are more focused on their power *in* the organisation rather than the capacity *of* their organisation to empower others and make change. These individuals seek control and accumulate power when they establish their own voting blocs. This means they 'own' a certain number of votes (that is, people). The other members of that group submit to the leader of the bloc and follow whatever that person decides. The party hierarchy knows it can rely on these blocs of votes, bringing a level of certainty to decision-making.

All these machinations are hidden from public view. The idea is you have your debates behind closed doors and then put a coherent position publicly – what is called 'holding the line'. Parties have been described to me as being like families: you may argue like crazy in private, but you will defend family members to the death if anyone from outside dares to criticise. Trading power through transactional exchanges is a reality and some say a necessary feature of politics. For old political animals the very idea that you would set aside self-interest, let go of control and share power for the benefit of others can be too threatening a prospect to contemplate.

When we look for examples of new political animals, we're unlikely to find them in political parties. But we can see changes emerging in workplaces and communities. Public policy and service design are a couple of areas where power relationships are being re-organised. Moving away from the top-down, expert-led, old power approaches, effort is shifting to bottom-up, community-led change. In one suburb that has high levels of disadvantage and poor health outcomes, organisational representatives were brought together to solve a specific problem: the high rate of ambulance call-outs was placing pressure on the city's public hospital. The group was made up of representatives from local community service organisations and government health officials and was tasked with finding solutions. Individual participants had to make a shift away from acting in the interest of their own organisation to acting in the interests of the whole community.

In a competitive funding environment, sometimes it was difficult to leave their own agendas at the door. But the group managed to cooperate among themselves, with other service providers in the area, and with local residents, to come up with a model of shared information about what services were available. This helped service providers make referrals and helped community members get the help they needed locally, making it less likely they would need to call an ambulance. In developing this new approach the group distributed power across a whole network of people, making a small shift from old power to new.

The tension between old and new politics is spilling out onto the streets around the world. The old political animals are holding onto their power for dear life. They will do whatever they can to maintain control and protect the status quo in a system that benefits their interests. Meanwhile the new political animals, like so-called 'leaderless' protesters in places like Hong Kong, are dispersing their power throughout networks as they take action in the interests of the common good.

The path between old and new politics is fluid. New political animals need to straddle both.

The path between old and new politics is fluid. New political animals need to straddle both, holding on to practices from the old politics while also embracing a new way of doing things. This means being strategic and playing the long game, as well as developing a new skill called 'political intelligence'.

Political intelligence

One way to think of political intelligence is: *emotional intelligence + power*. Emotional intelligence is typically defined as understanding your own and others' emotions – we will cover it in Chapter 3. Political intelligence adds to this a deep understanding of how power works and how to use it strategically. Also known as political savvy or political judgment, at its most basic political intelligence is knowing what to say and do, and when, to get the outcome you want.

In training your political animal you need to understand your personal, relational and collective power. Your personal power comes from your emotional intelligence, from being present in the moment and seeing clearly what's going on around you, and being able to choose your response to the situation. You also need to see and use your relational power (more in Chapters 4 and 5). Who is in your networks? What is the source of power for the people you are trying to influence? Then you can understand the resources you have to mobilise the collective power you have with others (see Chapter 6).

Political animals understand who they are acting for, who will help them get there and who will get in their way, and they know which tactics to pull out of their kit.

Political animals are strategic in their relationships. They have clarity about the outcomes they are trying to achieve in the short and long term. Fundamentally, they understand who they are acting for, who will help them get there and who will get in their way, and they know which tactics to pull out of their kit to mobilise or neutralise those actors.

Looking at relationships more strategically brings us to the concept of political capital. Political capital is the trust you build with others that allows you to influence outcomes and, like financial capital, it is a resource that can be saved up and spent.

To be politically intelligent is to bring all this knowledge like a lightning bolt into that moment where you have to make a quick judgment about what to say or do, and when. Timing is everything. Complex change takes time – and that's why you need to be prepared to play the long game (more in Chapter 7).

When we set out to change our world, we need to start with ourselves. The power flows from inside yourself, into your relationships and groups, and out into society. Growing your political intelligence enables you to make better decisions, to be a better colleague, community member and leader. When young employee Heidi opened her eyes to the power dynamics in the world around her, she changed the way she tackled the status quo. She consciously worked on her own emotional intelligence and, through trial and error, she came to understand and grow the source of her own power.

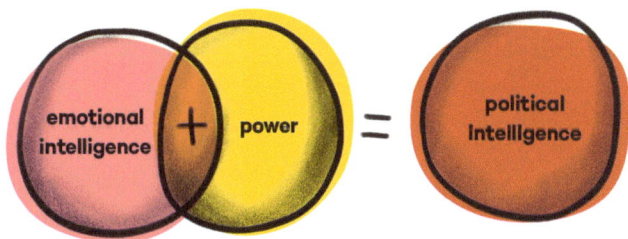

emotional intelligence + power = political intelligence

PRACTICE TIPS

Many millions of important decisions are made every day that affect people's lives. Some of those decisions aren't great – they lead to solutions that waste people's time, have huge costs and just don't work. To make change that benefits more people and the planet, more of us need to participate. Participating requires you to understand the unspoken power dynamics and to use your power for good. You need to expand your political intelligence and jump in: that way we'll change the game of politics from self-interest to self-awareness and from transactional to meaningful. New political animals like Heidi and the not-for-profit CEO, Nadia, are making sure power is visible and is shared in their organisations, and this helps everyone make good decisions that benefit people who are not like them.

The meaning of power

What is your first response to the word *power*?
What words do you associate with it?

How does the word make you feel?

What does *power* look like for you?
Does it bring up a particular person or image?

When were you in a situation where you felt powerless?
And powerful?

What needs to change for you to be more powerful?

Chapter 2:
Pay attention

Life moves pretty fast.
If you don't stop and look around
once in a while, you could miss it.

– FERRIS BUELLER

There's a reason why mindfulness is now a billion-dollar industry. Human beings aren't built for all this stimulation (cue SMS ping, scroll, tap, swipe left, funny cats). We're going crazy with all the distractions and we need an app to help us find calm. It has even reached a point where parents are having to be told to get off their phones to save their kids' lives. This is what German lifeguards had to do a few years ago when children were getting into trouble swimming at lakes and beaches because their parents were too absorbed in their phones to notice. This is quite serious, but perhaps it's not surprising, given how busy and distracted we've let ourselves become. We're working all hours of the day; we're running the kids around; we're 'on' all the time – online, on the ball, on the go. It has taken a global pandemic for people to stop, slow down and notice where they're putting their attention.

Paying attention to the world around you is the first lesson in training your political animal. There is so much information swirling around you that can help you make better decisions for a better world. But you'll miss it when you're frantic all the time and you're choosing to put your attention elsewhere. Someone else will use this valuable information, though, and sometimes use it against you and your cause. This is what happened to Ben when his boss was making moves to get rid of him.

Look around

Ben loved his job in a small television bureau where he worked as a camera assistant. It was busy, the team members got along okay and it was good fun. For three years he turned up to do his shifts, he didn't get too involved in anyone's business and took everyone at face value. That was until one day he got a phone call from the manager at HQ telling him he'd have to reapply for his job. He was pretty shocked; he thought

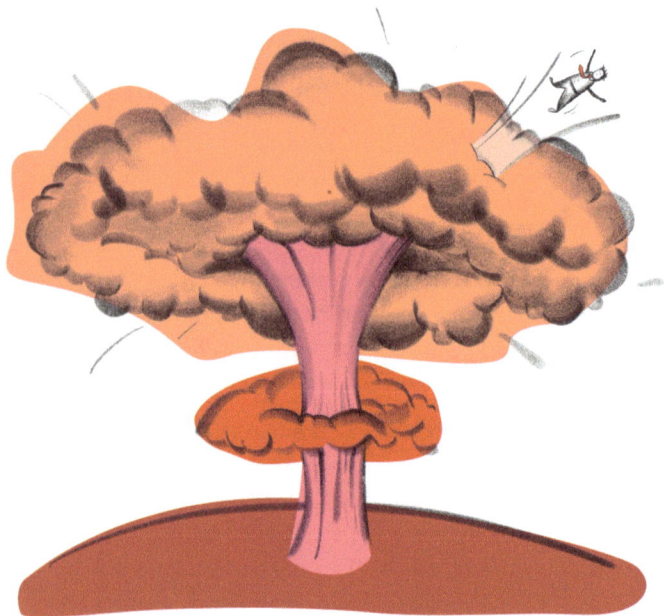

he had a regular gig and no one had told him otherwise – and there had been no conversations about his performance. He tried disputing the terms of his contract with management but got nowhere. He felt confused and, for the first time, suspicion crept in.

He began to wonder what his colleagues had been saying about him, and who he could trust. His confidence was rocked, but he had no other work to go to, so he went through the process of applying for his job and doing an interview. Later the manager sat him down and told him he was unsuccessful.

Ben didn't see it coming. He was never interested in office politics.

In that moment Ben looked around his workplace and saw an altogether different picture. He saw individuals within the team who were out for themselves. Being managed remotely from HQ left some staff feeling that they didn't have a voice and they were resentful about having to do things they didn't agree with. To protect their own positions some had cosied up to management, becoming best friends with the bosses. Along the way, as part of offering up budget savings, Ben became expendable. He was replaced by a younger, cheaper candidate.

Ben didn't see it coming. He'd come from a supportive workplace and was one of those people who was never interested in office politics, and in fact he actively dismissed the behaviour of colleagues as petty. He wasn't ambitious – he just wanted to turn up, do his job well, get along with people, and get paid. He didn't get involved in other people's games. What he discovered when he looked around was that other people weren't like him. They had different motivations, they had their own agendas, and they were much more tuned into the power dynamics of the place than he was. As a result of not paying attention, he was 'done over'.

Ben's experience of losing his job made him pay attention. In workplaces after that he was more aware of the people who were power players, and those who lacked emotional intelligence and were in it for themselves. He sought out healthy relationships, stayed private to people he didn't trust, and avoided doing things that could turn people against him. With this knowledge he became more powerful and was able to choose better responses. Ben became more of a political animal and went on to become a mentor to young people in his industry.

Boiling frogs

It took a huge jolt like getting sacked for Ben to pay attention. But it's also not surprising that he didn't see it coming. Human beings are pretty adaptable: we go with the flow, we get used to things like taking reusable bags to the supermarket, using hand sanitiser, wearing masks. Our adaptability can also be a problem. Think about a workplace that's toxic. You may have experienced one or certainly heard about this sort of environment. Our tolerance of toxic workplaces happens slowly over time. You get used to the gossip, the whispers in the corridors – you might even go along with what people say just to keep the peace. Then there's the closed door, with you on the other side, people looking askance, the curtain of the unspoken closing around you and it just doesn't feel right. Here you are, a boiling frog.

The analogy goes that you put a frog in a pot of cold water on the stove and turn up the temperature (don't try this at home). As the heat slowly increases, the frog adjusts its body temperature accordingly. Just when the water is about to reach boiling point, the frog is not able to adjust anymore, and at that point it decides to jump out. The problem is it can't jump because the poor wee fella has lost all its strength in adjusting to the rising water temperature. Very soon, sadly, it dies. So what killed the frog? 'The boiling water', you say. But alas, no, what killed the frog was its inability to decide when to jump out.

We don't choose a gossipy, sarcastic, back-stabbing workplace – it happens organically over time because individuals don't jump out in time.

One day in the toxic workplace scenario you wake up and you're physically ill with dread about having to turn up. But at that point you can't jump out. You've lost all your strength and your confidence and your sense of yourself. The toxic workplace didn't make you sick; you made yourself sick by not knowing when to leave. You haven't used your power to choose your response to the situation. It can be pretty confronting to be the one who goes against the flow and stands up to the perpetrators of an unhealthy workplace. But when you remain silent or you join in, you are complicit. We don't choose a gossipy, sarcastic, back-stabbing workplace

– it happens organically over time because individuals don't jump out in time.

There are plenty of examples in everyday life of things we wouldn't choose but that we get used to. Think surveillance cameras. Walk through any city or town now and there are CCTV cameras everywhere. It seems lame to even mention it now; they are so commonplace you probably don't even notice them. But imagine if years ago our governments had asked us, 'What's the best way to keep us all safe?', would we have said, 'Put cameras on every corner and street pole'? It probably wouldn't have been our first thought (well-resourced social services would have been mine). We didn't choose eyes everywhere, it just kind of happened. It's not even that we didn't notice; we did notice, we just felt too powerless to challenge it. The tsunami of fear that washed through society after 9/11 was too big to stop. Then we just got used to it and changed our behaviour, making sure we went home from the pub just before we were tempted to do that stupid (but probably pretty funny) thing we could have got away with in the good old days.

We are boiling frogs in so many ways. It's possible to assume things have always been like this. Take inequality as an example. We didn't always live in such an unequal society. In fact, inequality has been around for about 10,000 years, since *homo sapiens* stayed put, grew crops and put fences up to keep out the riff raff. But the gap in wealth has never been as huge as it is now. According to Oxfam, the world's 2000 billionaires have more wealth than 60 per cent of the entire population of the planet (4.6 billion people). This

was before the global pandemic, during which those billionaires got even richer. If we'd been asked, would we have chosen this scenario? 'Hell yeah, let's concentrate wealth in the hands of the one per cent.' No we wouldn't choose this. It just happened that way.

Except it didn't just happen. Like so many of our broken systems that no longer serve the greater good, wealth inequality is the result of millions of decisions made every day by individual human beings. And just as we have been participants in the construction of this system, we can participate in the creation of an alternative. For us all to make different decisions we first have to wake up.

Stop sleepwalking

Sure, it's easier to just turn up every day and go with the flow. Many people do. But what if we woke up? What if something major happened in our lives to jolt us out of our comfort zone, to show us that we can live a different way? Like maybe a global pandemic? When we stop sleepwalking all our senses are alive. It's like when you land in a new place. You walk out of the hotel in the morning and you notice everything. The sounds of the birds, the air on your skin, the colours, shadows and the light, the aromas of new food, the vibe of the place.

It's the same when you start a new job. Walking into the office or onto the workshop floor on the first day, you're tuned in to everything that's going on. The way people talk, what they say, who hangs out with who, how the furniture is arranged, the processes that don't make sense. You can make decisions pretty quickly about what you like, and also see clearly what's not working. That's why, if managers want a reality check, if they want to find out what's going on (and going wrong) in their organisation, they should ask the new person. The newbies will have a unique perspective and notice things other workers will no longer see. But there's not much time – it doesn't take long for the new person to stop seeing; soon they too will become part of the furniture.

Political animals don't sleepwalk. **They see and hear everything. They move quietly through the corridors, dropping in on colleagues for a casual friendly chat and walk away with the key piece of the puzzle they need to work out what's going on.**

Improve your attention in three ways

To make better decisions, to challenge accepted truths and make change that matters, you need to develop three skills in your training:

Look under the surface

Really listen

See the whole picture

Look under the surface

A lot of what we need to pay attention to sits under the surface in the murky realm of 'culture'. Culture is a woolly subject that is made up of all the things that we can't see and can't control, but which have a huge influence on the way we interact and the decisions we make. It is typically defined as 'the way we do things round here' and is made visible in what we do and what we say – our behaviour and attitudes.

When we're making important decisions and solving problems we often only see the tip of the iceberg. That's because we're busy and working under pressure, so we don't have the time or space to consider what's under the surface. It's easier anyway to put most of our energy into that one-tenth that we can see and control. We make 'to do' lists, come up with processes, strategies, plans, policies, KPIs, spreadsheets – all the busy work that constitutes 'the doing'. As a consequence of this busy 'doing' we don't pay as much attention to the nine-tenths of the iceberg under the surface. But we should, because this is where the juicy stuff is – what we call 'the being'. All the complexity of human relationships lives here: the culture of the team, our values systems, collective stories and vision, and, of course, the power dynamics.

When we don't see all of the dynamics going on under the surface we can end up fixing the wrong problem.

When we don't see all of the dynamics going on under the surface we can end up fixing the wrong problem. We run for a quick fix, what we call a technical or process solution, rather than a more complicated cultural or adaptive solution that requires us to change something in ourselves and our relationships. In 2015, the Speaker of the Australian House of Representatives got caught out taking an 80-kilometre helicopter ride to a political party function at the taxpayers' expense. When she was found out it caused outrage in the media and was deemed an act that failed to 'pass the pub test'. The response of the government was to conduct a review into the parliamentary entitlements system. The review came out with a range of recommendations for reducing ambiguity and responding better to alleged misuse of entitlements. There were many suggestions for changes to processes and rules – a lot of technical solutions for what was in large part a cultural problem.

Imagine, instead, if this question had been asked: 'What sort of culture makes behaviour like this okay?' Imagine if we'd been invited into a conversation about the culture of privilege in our political class. Coming up with new processes and rules is an easy, quick fix but it doesn't necessarily address the real causes, and this means the solutions don't work and they don't last. Which, of course, is exactly what happened when it was revealed, just a few years later in early 2020, that Australian MPs across political parties had been using taxpayers' funds to attend party fundraisers.

The employment services system in Australia has been broken for a while, the holes patched up like an old, worn-out, inflatable mattress. There were many things wrong with the rules and processes, but the heart of the problem lay in a flawed assumption that people don't want to work. The entire system, and all its compliance requirements, was built on the idea that the clients weren't to be trusted because they didn't really want a job anyway. The division of society into those who want to work and those who don't is reinforced by political leaders using language like 'lifters and leaners'. The impact on human beings of an assumption like this is profound. It generates feelings of shame, humiliation and stigma for people in the system. In talking to people about their experiences with their local employment service agencies, one young guy called Jake put it clearly to me when he said, 'I get the impression they think we lie all the time'.

In the 2018 national review into employment services the panel listened to the voices of hundreds of users of the system – job seekers, employers and service providers. Panel members found that most Australians do want to work, and in fact they called their report, *I Want to Work*. They set out a path that addressed both the technical and cultural problems with solutions that invited us to imagine a day when someone like Jake can walk into his local employment services office and feel trusted that he is telling the truth. Imagine that?

New political animals see what's going on under the surface. They diagnose the cultural problems as well as the technical problems. As a result they make better decisions and create meaningful change that lasts.

See the whole picture

The second skill for new political animals to develop in paying attention is to see the whole picture. It's too easy these days to think everyone sees the world the same way you do. We are drawn to views that affirm our own. Social media has propelled us into these bubbles where we bounce around like Thunderbirds in echo chambers of people who agree with us. This means we only see part of the picture, not the whole picture, and this has serious implications for good decision-making. New political animals need to be able to get out of their own shoes and see the problem from different points of view.

Take the example of a group of suburban parents who have come together to lobby for a new school in their city. They're angry at the lack of public education options for their kids. They are suspicious that the government has already made a decision to expand one of the local schools instead of building a new one.

Rather than a genuine conversation, the government's community consultation on the issue is perceived as going through the motions. Operating as political animals, the outraged parents put their energy into petitioning local MPs, generating media stories and motivating others to join their cause through social media. This is the way you get heard, and in a world where those who yell the loudest get the most attention, they may very well be successful. But something else is happening: they create a bubble with everyone who agrees with them and this stops them seeing the whole picture. Worse than that, they form a tribe and demonise anyone who disagrees. The government becomes the enemy. The existing local school community becomes the enemy. And the opportunity for an open, creative conversation about the best solution gets lost.

Political animals may set out acting in their own interest (the education of their own kids), but they need to expand their awareness to see the whole picture (the education of other people's kids, now and for future generations). In this case there are two critical voices that need to be heard before any decisions are made about local schools. One is the voice of marginalised parents. They may not be as educated and articulate as our outraged parents, and they may lack the confidence to participate because of negative experiences in their own schooling. The other critical voice is the children themselves. They are the ones who will actually attend the school for a good part of their lives. When new political animals bring a range of diverse voices into the conversation, surprising things can happen. They may discover that education is not about new buildings, but about the culture of the school and the relationships that form – it takes a village.

When we're trying to make change for the common good we can end up stumbling over cliffs if we're blinded by our own world view.

It's entirely normal that we look out from the centre of our world through our own unique lens. It's like wearing our own special eyeglasses created from our own set of judgments, habits, assumptions, and the stories we tell ourselves about what we see and experience: big business = greedy; unemployed people = lazy; politicians = liars. When we're trying to make change for the common good we can end up stumbling over cliffs if we're blinded by our own world view. To make the best decisions, to make a change that matters in your community, you need to take your glasses off. Deliberately seek out people who aren't like you, with different points of view. Find a devil's advocate to test your ideas with – someone who can give you a reality check. To really understand the perspectives of others and see the whole picture, you need to get good at the next skill on our 'pay attention' list, the most underrated skill of politics: listening.

Really listen

There's a little story made in the year 1752 by a Buddhist monk called Soyer Shakr: Two men were walking over a crowded marketplace. Suddenly one exclaimed, 'Listen to the lovely sound of that cricket'. But the other could not hear. 'How can you hear a cricket in all this noise?' he asked his companion. The first man did not explain but took a coin out of his pocket and dropped it. A dozen people began to look about them. 'We hear', he said, 'what we listen for.'

This is a story I had pinned to my wall when I was a teenager. I still can't find the source, but this idea that we wander the world hearing only what we listen for has always intrigued me. It happens all the time. If you are sick of your job and ready to move on you will hear all the negative comments your colleagues make about the place, and you probably won't register the positive things. It makes sense; we can't possibly hear everything – we need some sort of filter and it may as well be our own bias.

Here's a familiar scenario: you're in conversation with someone, they're telling you about something that happened to them. In your head you're thinking, 'I've got a better story than that'. They take a mistimed breath and you seize the silence, jumping in with your own blistering anecdote. And then when you've shared your story the other person leaps back in with their version. A lot of conversations are like this – a tennis match. And what's wrong with that? Humans thrive on story; we have done since the cave folk were grunting at drawings in the dirt. It's okay to exchange stories like this as a way of connecting, sure. Except it's not. Well, not if you want to change anything. That takes a different type of conversation, one with listening in it. Real listening. This is the third skill.

A seasoned political animal called Chris thought she took people as they came until she found herself in a high-pressure environment in a group whose perspectives and background were different to hers. She was frustrated by an autocratic chair who would shut down conversation. She found herself judging and labelling him in her head, so that when he said something she disagreed with it validated her (low) opinion of him. This meant she stopped listening. It didn't take long for her to work out that not only was it important to hear what he was saying, but to also understand his perspective if she was to achieve positive outcomes for the people she represented.

In influencing, the best way to be heard is to listen.

For new political animals to understand issues deeply, to make better decisions and shape the thinking of other decision-makers, they need to know where people are coming from. You won't find that out while your ego is clambering around in your head and you're barking your opinions at them. When you stay quiet and truly listen, you can find out a whole lot of useful information that can help your cause. Political animals listen out for any snippets that can improve their position. They float around like sponges soaking in all the information, assembling it into something meaningful and handing it over when it can be most powerful. In influencing, the best way to be heard is to listen.

To achieve real change, new political animals need to bring compassion and curiosity to their listening, not just to progress their cause, but to lift up those around them. Think about a time when you've had a great teacher or great coach – it's like they hold the space for you and help you see your own potential. They don't jump in with their advice or their own opinion. Instead they ask really powerful questions that help you have insight and work out the answers yourself.

New political animals need to be able to hold their own views lightly and listen with genuine openness to others. Really listening is a respectful act. When people are heard they allow links of trust to be built. This can happen not just between individuals, but on the scale of whole systems and communities. The government in Seoul, South Korea, demonstrated the value it places on listening in a real, physical way. It built a giant ear-shaped sculpture outside the city hall. Anyone can pass by and tell the government what they think and their voices are broadcast to the civil servants inside.

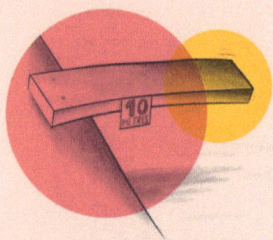

PRACTICE TIPS

It's hard to pay attention to the important stuff when we're distracted all the time. We get used to the way things are and sometimes it takes a jolt for us to stop sleepwalking and look around. When we look, we may not like what we see and want to change it. To achieve change, political animals need to develop three important skills: looking under the surface so that they understand the culture and can find adaptive solutions; seeing the whole picture by getting out of their own bubble and into other people's shoes; and really listening so they can understand others, build trust and find out what's really going on. New political animal Ben doesn't get 'done over' anymore and he shares what he has learned about power with younger people in his industry to help them make better choices.

Notice the boiling frogs

Think about the world around you, from inside your house to your neighbourhood and beyond. What has changed over the years that you haven't really paid attention to? You might come up with things like:

- apples that come pre-shined
- people sleeping in doorways at the train station
- bushfires at the start of September.

Fix the right problem

When you are trying to resolve challenges, spend time on the question, 'What is the problem we are trying to solve?' A good diagnosis of the problem will lead you to the most appropriate solutions. Will it be fixed by a new process or rule, or do you need to focus on the culture – on values and attitudes?

Get a different perspective

Jump out of your own bubble and see things from a different perspective. Walk a new path, take a different bus, read an article by someone you don't like. What would someone who has a very different set of beliefs to you say about your situation?

Take minutes of the unspoken

Hone your skills in paying attention. Next time you're in a meeting, pay attention to what is unsaid. Where do people usually sit? What is the body language like? Who holds power in the room? What's happening to the energy level - who lifts it and who drains it? How do you feel at the end of the meeting compared to the beginning?

Listen to understand

Next time you're in a conversation, notice when you're primed ready to jump in with your own story. Instead, stop and really listen, ask a question or two. You might find you don't need to tell your story at all.

Chapter 3:
Change yourself

Everyone thinks of changing the world,
but nobody thinks of changing himself.
– LEO TOLSTOY

Which task seems more daunting: changing the whole
world or changing yourself? Some people can live their
whole lives without making that scary turn inwards to
look at who they are. They can pass by mirrors without
even a sideways glance and can find plenty to do to
avoid any chance of an awkward quiet moment alone
with themselves. It would be nice to be a completed
project with nothing new to learn. But no one is a full
stop – we're a work in progress until we die. So you may
be standing there stuck knee-high in mud with your
arms folded and nothing more to learn, but the world
is spinning at lightning speed around you. And you're
missing out on that great trip to understanding who
you really are. Tolstoy also said, 'There can be only one
permanent revolution – a moral one: the regeneration of
the inner man'. This lesson for the new political
animal is about being open to changing yourself.

Political animals can no longer get away with staying
stuck in their own skin, denying responsibility and
ranting that it's someone else's fault. They need to shake
off their old defensive habits and stop clinging on for
dear life to their beliefs and ideas. It's time to get out of
the mud, be curious about why you say things and do
things the way you do, and be kind to yourself as you
step out into creating a better world – and a better you.

Get unstuck

Human beings are creatures of habit. We do our morning tasks in the same order – shower and dress, eat breakfast, brush teeth (or something like that). We travel the same way to work each day, have lunch at the same time, put the cups back in the same place. Our habits give us comfort in this crazy world – they help us feel like we're in control, creating a sense of order. But there are other types of habits that aren't so good for us. These are our habits of thought, the stories we tell ourselves and the judgments we make about ourselves. We can be our own harshest critic and this can stop us making the changes we need to make, for ourselves and the world around us. The first step for political animals to change themselves is to notice their unhappy habits, and this can be like going through a new door, as Luke discovered.

Luke had trouble getting his kids to go to bed. Every night the boys would come back out to the lounge room and every night Luke would yell at them, leap up off the couch and storm down the hallway as they scampered back to their rooms. He didn't feel great about this routine, but he didn't know there could be another way. It's one of those habits we can all get stuck in when we're tired at the end of the day. Luke named this one up as one of his unhappy habits in a workshop, and that night he tried something different. When the kids wandered back into the lounge room Luke quietly got up, held them both by the hand and walked down the hallway without a word. He gently tucked them into bed with a kiss on the forehead. In shock, the elder boy said, 'What's wrong, Dad? You're not yelling at us'. Noticing the unhappy habit and changing it was good for Luke and his boys.

First he noticed it, then he chose a different response, then other things changed.

When you're stuck, you don't realise you're stuck, so you'll respond to situations the same way you always have. When you're free, you have more choices, and you're more likely to see the situation from other perspectives than just your own. For us to choose a different response we have to be curious about ourselves, about our own behaviour. Luke was prompted to wonder why he yelled at the kids every night and how unhappy that behaviour made him feel. First he noticed it, then he chose a different response, then other things changed. Rather than see bedtime as a chore to get through at the end of a busy day, Luke and his partner made it a priority. They took turns to sit with the kids, listen to them and read books. It didn't always work out, and when the stress built up he slipped back into old habits, but he noticed and knew what he had to do to change it.

The path to happier habits is neither straight nor smooth. It is like a rollercoaster with *Stuck* at one end and *Free* at the other and all the curly bits in between. It loops back on itself, slows down in some places and plummets at breakneck speed at others. Just when you think you know yourself well and you're making healthy choices, *Bam!* You're knocked down by a global pandemic. When the stress hits you're more likely to be on automatic and the unhappy habits creep back. But if you've done some work on yourself already, it won't be long before you notice you're in an unhealthy place and you get yourself back on track. The journey from *Stuck* to *Free* was explained by the manager of an emergency housing centre who helped people experiencing homelessness: 'At the beginning they come in with their hand out asking, "What can you do for me?" and over time we work with them and then they ask, "What can I do to help?"'

Political animals are at their best when they take the time to notice the noise in their heads. Pay attention to your unhappy habits and the stories you tell yourself – the many ways in which you are stuck. Then let them go, like blowing through a dandelion. It takes practice, perhaps even a lifetime of unlearning. But the effort is worth it when we see the world as new, like a child does. The challenge for political animals is to keep noticing, even when life gets stressful and change gets hard. That takes a high degree of emotional intelligence.

Emotional intelligence

We need to consciously and deliberately work on being more emotionally intelligent.

More than 4.5 billion humans use the internet. There are tens of thousands of online searches every second, and billions of searches each day. Pretty much anyone can find out whatever they want and learn whatever they want online. We have travelled a million miles from the preacher in the pulpit being the holder of all knowledge for the village. We no longer work in a world where the manager always knows more than the workers, or even where the teacher always knows more than the students. So it follows that our value as a human being comes less from what we know and more from who we are. It's not good enough anymore for political animals to blunder through, staying stuck in old habits, oblivious to the impact of their behaviour on others. We need to consciously and deliberately work on being more emotionally intelligent.

A guru of emotional intelligence, Daniel Goleman, was talking about these concepts towards the end of last century. In one of his many good books on the subject, *Working with Emotional Intelligence*, he said we would be judged not so much by our technical abilities or intelligence (IQ), but by 'how well we handle ourselves and each other' (EQ). In Goleman's model the competencies we all need include self-awareness – which is about recognising your own and other people's emotions – and self-management – which is about regulating your own emotions when you engage with others.

These ideas are pretty familiar now, as employers appoint new staff based on how well they demonstrate self-awareness, and kids in schools are given tools for developing a growth mindset. Even a former Australian Prime Minister, Malcolm Turnbull, talked about EQ on the first day of his new job in an interview on ABC TV: 'The important thing is to have the emotional intelligence and the empathy and the imagination that enables you to walk in somebody else's shoes ... Emotional intelligence is probably the most important asset for anyone in my line of work'.

It's not too difficult to spot someone with low emotional intelligence. Imagine a politician facing tough questions from the media about a situation where they behaved badly. Two things will happen. First, they will be stuck in self. They won't have the ability to see the situation from someone else's perspective,

or the broader context. Second, they will be defensive. They won't have the ability to take responsibility for their part in the situation and they will use tactics like denial and blaming others. Contrast this with a person of higher emotional intelligence and you'll find someone who may not even be in the situation, but if they are, they will see it from the perspective of the people impacted. Then they will take responsibility, if not for the situation itself, then for their own response, zooming out to the broader context and putting their own needs and ego aside to make a decision for the greater good.

If you can be yourself you've got it made.

For old political animals the truism is, 'If you can fake sincerity you've got it made'. But in the tell-all world of social media it's getting harder to be inauthentic. Under the lights of constant scrutiny, inconsistency and hypocrisy are being called out. We are shifting to a new truism: 'If you can be yourself you've got it made'. This means new political animals need to not hide their vulnerabilities. They need to say they don't know or they're afraid, because when they do this they invite others to open up themselves. The old politics is a game where people say one thing and do another, or say one thing to one person and something different to another. New political animals are changing the game of politics to one where the players act with integrity, and integrity is what you do when no one else is looking. We're at the point of peak fakery; it is laid bare, oozing from the White House and Downing Street and Canberra. The new wave is sincerity, so let's get real.

There are a lot of tools around to help you on a path to higher levels of emotional intelligence, and here's the catch, *the work is never done*. There's no certificate waiting for you at the end of your EQ training. It's not like you can turn up to a graduation ceremony with an elite bunch of emotionally intelligent humans and peer down from your enlightened cloud on the rest of us. Instead it's a daily slog, and because we're human we stumble, we fall down and get back up, get another scar and learn something new about ourselves. But if you're open, if you're prepared, as Walt Whitman said, to 'Be curious, not judgmental', then you're on your way to being a new political animal who makes more effective decisions every day.

Head, heart and body

How do you make a decision? Do you mull it over for days, analysing every angle? Do you go with how it feels? Do you jump quickly and regret it later? When you're asked for a response to something, do you say, 'I'll think about it'? Do you listen to your heart? Do you go with your gut instinct? Noticing how you make decisions can give you a valuable insight into yourself, and get you on the path to making better ones.

There are many models for working yourself out. Search up personality types on the web and you can find a whole range of tools to diagnose yourself as a bird, a colour, a series of letters or a number. The one I'm using here comes from the Enneagram personality system and focuses on the three centres of intelligence. The idea is we don't just make decisions in our brains – our whole body is involved. There are 100 million neurons in your intestines and 40 thousand neurons in your heart that can process information.

Each of us is capable of thinking in all three ways — head, heart and body — but we tend to lean strongly towards one of them.

Each of us is capable of thinking in all three ways — head, heart and body — but we tend to lean strongly towards one of them. These centres of intelligence are the filter through which we see the world. We tend to trust the thoughts that come from our preferred centre and don't trust, or avoid, what the other centres are telling us. Knowing the differences between the three centres helps us understand ourselves and each other (thanks to the Global Leadership Foundation for the following outline).

In the head, or thinking centre, we make decisions based on knowledge, reason and logic — our insight. People who are dominated by their head centre are comfortable in their inner world and seek a feeling of security. They are more likely to think before speaking, walking away from situations wishing they had said more than they did. They may be more focused on the future than are people dominated by the other centres. If you tend to feel hassled when information is dumped on you and you have to give a quick response, you may be dominated by your head centre.

In the heart, or feeling centre, we make decisions based on our emotions – what we are feeling – our intuition. People who are dominated by their heart centre are comfortable with their outer world (people, things, events) and seek love and approval from others. They are more likely to read people's mannerisms, body language and energy. They tend to be more focused on the past, and may be more nostalgic, than people coming from the other centres. If you find yourself getting worked up about the tone of someone's email, you may be dominated by your heart centre.

In the body, or doing centre, we make decisions based on our senses and experiences in the world around us – our instinct. People who are dominated by their body centre are comfortable in the here and now and they seek independence. They are more likely to speak before thinking, walking away from situations wishing they hadn't said what they did. They tend to be more focused on the present than people working from the other centres are. If you get impatient with planning and want to move quickly to action you may be dominated by your body centre.

When they set out to make better decisions, political animals need to have their three centres of intelligence in balance. When you know you are dominated by your body centre and are more likely to rush to action, it is important that you hit the pause button, go for a walk and have a think about it. When you know you are dominated by your head centre and can overthink things, it is liberating to take off before you are ready, and accept what happens. When you know you are dominated by your heart centre and can get caught up in the emotions of an issue, it is helpful to acknowledge that the feelings will pass, and do something practical like dig up your garden. The best way to get your centres in balance is to have people around you who can give you a different perspective. Another way we are different from each other is in our values.

Check your values

Liz was a senior executive in a medium-sized organisation. She had a very nice salary package that included a car, phone and excellent superannuation. She had the autonomy she craved, had avoided the curse of being micro-managed, yet somehow she came to be utterly miserable at work. She was filled with dread as she rolled into the grey basement every morning. It wasn't long before she found herself withdrawing, avoiding people and closing her door, trudging through her job doing just enough to make sure no one would notice how unhappy she was. One day a friend sent her a quiz about comparing your personal values with those of your organisation. In a quiet moment she tapped out her answers. She nearly fell off her chair when she saw the results. She valued creativity, family, fairness and making a difference. But she identified her organisation's values as competition, efficiency, accountability and profit. Completely different. There on the screen was the source of her unhappiness. And she hadn't even realised. She resigned not long after.

We all live by certain values that are important to us. Some stay with us from childhood and others we pick up and change through life.

When you're making decisions and everything feels like it's in a state of flux there is something you can rely on, and that is your values. Put simply, values are what we value. We all live by certain values that are important to us. Some stay with us from childhood and others we pick up and change through life. Values can come from our parents, school, our friends, colleagues, and the place and culture we live in. Our values guide whether we read the *Herald Sun* or *The Guardian*, whether we watch *The Block* or *Grand Designs*. Without a clear sense of our values we might find ourselves floating like a feather on a breeze, not knowing where to land. Decisions are harder without an anchor that stops us trying to please everyone.

Values sit under the surface of the iceberg that we talked about in Chapter 2. They form a big part of our 'being' – who we are as individuals – but we don't really talk about them. It's worth taking a minute to reflect on yourself growing up. What did your family value? What behaviour was praised and what was criticised? Was it about winning or having a go? Was it about holding your own in an argument or making peace? Was it about letting your feelings show or being stoic? Values are made visible in our choices and our behaviours. Often we only pay attention to our values when we're annoyed by people or when things blow up. Different values may also explain why working in our organisation just doesn't feel right.

We don't all have the option of leaving a workplace that clashes with our values, like Liz did, but we do have the power to make our values visible every day. And we have the capacity for compassion and to understand when our values clash with the values of others. Political animals make better decisions when they use their values as the foundation. This is not to say every decision will line up perfectly with your values, sometimes you need to be pragmatic, but your values can guide the way you communicate your decision. Values are your anchor when you're dealing with the changes around you.

Dealing with change

How are you at dealing with change? There is an old Chinese proverb that goes, 'At times of great winds some build bunkers while others build windmills'. Which path do you choose? It often depends on the change of course, and whether you're in control of it or whether it's out of your control. When the pandemic hit, many parents in my community pulled their children out of school. At the time there was an overwhelming need to feel in control of something when everything else felt out of control. It was only when people felt secure in their bunkers that they could hoist up their windmills.

No baby is born with a strategic plan for their life. We all have to live with complexity and uncertainty.

Change is all around us and is happening faster than ever before. Imagine it like a flow of sand through your hands. We let some change through because it makes sense, or we realise we can't stop it. But other change doesn't feel right so we have to hold up our hand and create a resistance that sends the flow in a different direction. Human beings try to gain a sense of control through things like writing lists and plans, but the truth is, no baby is born with a strategic plan for their life. We all have to live with complexity and uncertainty – without a script. When you are setting out to lead change you must be able to let go of this attachment to certainty and be adaptable. You need to be able to read the signs and act on them, then notice what happens and adjust.

This is what the entire population of planet earth has done as we have experienced the global pandemic together. It has been said that while we're not all in the same boat, we are all on the same ocean. The safety of our boat depends on lots of things, including our age, health profile, socio-economic status, and our ability to deal with rapid and profound change. We get better at dealing with change when we're open to changing ourselves.

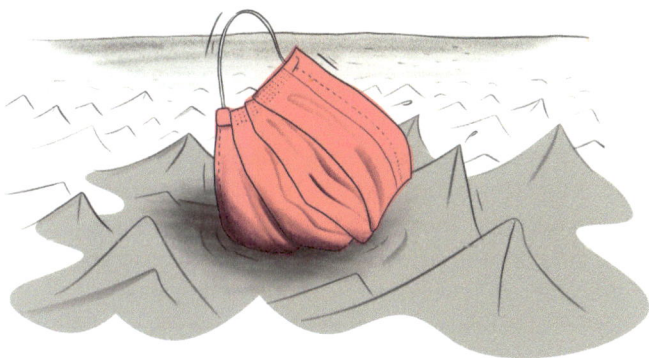

New habits

Being a political animal takes practice. It requires a shift in your mindset, and that starts with noticing your habits – your habits of thought – and your behaviour.

So you read a book like this one and maybe you get excited. You go to a workshop and you get inspired. You hear someone's story and you're motivated to change. There's a better world out there and it's just within your grasp – you're reaching … reaching … oh actually you can't be bothered. Grab the remote, click on a streaming service and spend the next hour looking for something to watch. Old habits are hard to break. So I'm making this as simple as possible, I really am. Being a political animal takes practice. It requires a shift in your mindset, and that starts with noticing your habits – your habits of thought – and your behaviour.

So choose one of your habits. Maybe you keep looking at your phone while people are talking to you. Put your phone down, look at them, listen, ask them a question. Another habit you may have is when someone comes to you with an idea you automatically think of things that could go wrong. So stop. Instead of saying 'No but …', say 'Yes and …'. Maybe you are quick to judge; there's a voice in your head that says, 'This guy's an idiot'. Stop. Be curious about why he says what he does; ask him a question. Try moving towards the people who are different to you instead of away. If you are a boss and your staff always come to you for the answers, don't make it easy. Ask them what they think and help them learn and grow. They'll probably have the answers anyway, just not the confidence to say them.

You need that energy for doing the good stuff, so try asking yourself: 'Who will I be when things don't work out?' When it all goes pear-shaped will you learn about yourself, and laugh at the absurdity of it all?

When we're on this journey of living deliberately and using our power to change our world, things won't always work out. When we step out and take a risk, like asking a different question and challenging an accepted truth, we can be left feeling humiliated and demoralised, and want to give up. This is because we're human and we feel good when things go well and bad when they don't. Our new habits of thought have to include being kinder to ourselves. That inner voice that shouts at you when you've done something wrong takes a lot of your energy. You need that energy for doing the good stuff, so try asking yourself: 'Who will I be when things don't work out?' When it all goes pear-shaped will you learn about yourself, and laugh at the absurdity of it all?

PRACTICE TIPS

We're not going to make good decisions and create a better world when we're stuck in old habits. Before anything else, political animals need to work on themselves. Like our 'stuck' dad, Luke, putting his kids to bed, you need to notice the habits that make you unhappy and you need to change them. Like senior executive Liz, stuck in an organisation she hates, you need to make decisions that line up with your own values. For political animals the path to higher emotional intelligence is not difficult; it starts with being curious about yourself, understanding with kindness why you do and say things a certain way. Use whatever tools you like to understand yourself better, the important thing is to be able to stop in the moment and make the best decision. It is this conscious choice to change yourself that will propel you into changing your world.

Reflect on your morning

What happens in your morning routine? How do you start each day? What about your habits of thought? What stories do you tell yourself as you get moving and thinking about your day? Do you have worries or fears? What are you looking forward to? Noticing your internal dialogue can help you work out which thoughts drain your energy and which ones energise you. Then you can decide which ones to hold onto and which ones to let go.

What do you value?

Think about a person who has had a big impact on your life. What advice did they give you?

What is a favourite book, movie, song or poem that has meaning for you?

What experience has really shaped your life? What value did it leave you with?

Our values are made visible in our decisions and our actions. What specific things do you do each day that show you are living by your values? What could you do more of?

Practise curiosity over judgment

Think about a difficult situation you're facing. It might be conflict with a person, something that causes you to worry. What is the story you tell yourself about this situation? What assumptions do you hold about it? What judgments are you making?

Now ask yourself what if the opposite were true? What is an alternative story? What do you need to let go of? What do you need to learn?

Chapter 4:
Make friends

I get by with a little help from my friends.
– LENNON/MCCARTNEY

The archetypal hero story is about the brave individual who takes on the world. We know these people from our own recent history. Greta Thunberg started as a solo climate change protester outside the Swedish Parliament and went on to become the voice of a generation, telling the adults of the world, 'I want you to panic'. We know the image of the lone Chinese man standing in front of the tank in Tiananmen Square in 1989. These individuals have courage. They disrupt the status quo through their public actions and they give others permission to do the same. They wake us up. Maybe you are that person too – unafraid to speak truth to power. Or maybe you want to be more like that person? Are you the new board member who puts their hand up at the first meeting and says you've noticed the tension in the room and asks what that's about?

In that moment you may be welcomed as a breath of fresh air who helps the group fix their dysfunctional relationships, or quite possibly you will be branded a renegade who is dangerous, and no one will speak to you.

The truth is we know these stories of individual courage because they are rare. Most of us are not brave enough to challenge accepted truths in such a public way. It is highly risky to put your head above the parapet, especially in today's unforgiving, unforgetting world of social media. But when we step out with others, with allies by our side, we are braver.

Friends you can rely on

Making change is hard, especially when you're taking on powerful people with entrenched views. To do that you need friends – sometimes many friends – and most times a powerful friend or two. Most importantly, these friends of yours need to be reliable.

As a political adviser I enjoyed questioning accepted truths – within our organisation and in society in general. Once, after a particularly gruelling period of controversial law reform, where our own leader's office had been leaking to the media against my minister, I decided to confront some of the perpetrators. On the Monday after the laws had passed the parliament, I called two colleagues and told them I was going to raise the issue in our team meeting later that day. I asked them to back me up and they said they would. As I walked into the meeting my hands were shaking and my throat was dry. I was extremely nervous, but determined to not let this period pass without comment. I cleared my throat and spoke up, naming up the destructive behaviour and asking that we all talk about it openly so we could rebuild trust. I was pretty happy with my mini speech and sat back waiting for my colleagues to speak in support. I waited. Silence. I looked over at them and they had their heads down, suddenly finding urgent papers to read. I waited. No one spoke up to support me. I was left, as they say, 'swinging in the breeze'.

If you want to challenge accepted truths ... you need a powerful network that you can rely on.

Creating the sort of change we want to see relies on us building real connections with other human beings. Relationships are the net that holds us up, and when it breaks we fall. In my story I learned that I had chosen the wrong people to back me, and I had also underestimated how low the level of trust was in my organisation. Choosing your allies can be a bit trial and error. You need to spend time listening and observing and finding common ground with people, so that when you ask them to stand with you they also get something out of it.

If you want to challenge accepted truths on a regular basis or in a big way, you need a powerful network that you can rely on when you step out to make change. For political animals, building strategic relationships must become the foundation of their plan, and this requires them to give their trust away and see what happens.

Trust is a gift you give

It was the thirty-third president of the United States, Harry S Truman, who famously said, 'You want a friend in Washington? Get a dog'. It's a simple line that paints a dark, cynical portrait of the friendless world of politics. Take a cursory look from above at the way old political animals behave and you see a web of handshakes: I'll do this for you if you do this for me. Support me here and I'll support you next time (maybe). It's the deal-making that gets things done. This all works fine in a linear world, but that's not where we live. We live in a complex world. We're happy to participate in a deal with our optometrist where we can get two for the price of one. That's a transaction, and we do those every day. But if we're trying to make change that matters, that's a whole different conversation. We've got to go beyond the transactional and into the meaningful, and that takes trust.

In her inspiring book, *Unlikely Leaders*, Cathy Burke talks about trust as a gift you give. She says, 'Trust is not something earned by the recipient, it is an act of generosity that rewards itself'. It's a challenging idea. Most people have experienced betrayal in some form - have had the trust they'd given away thrown back at them. The parent who breaks a promise to a child, the boyfriend who cheated, the friend who shared your secret, the colleague who didn't stand up when you needed them to. Trust is a fragile thing that doesn't take much to break, but it can take a lot to fix.

The signs of low trust in organisations are obvious when you take a look. Closed doors. Whispers in corners. Being suspicious about people's motives. Triangle communications where it is more common to complain sideways to a colleague rather than talk directly to the person you have the issue with. These are all features of the way old political animals operate. When the organisational culture is healthier and levels of trust are higher, there are smaller gaps between what is said and what is done. Working from home during the pandemic was a huge experiment in trust for many organisations. Managers had to give away the gift of trust to employees who were working remotely. They learned that when staff feel there is trust in their own ability, and trust between them and others, they pay back the gift through higher productivity.

Building trust takes time. It requires you to be human, vulnerable and to share personal information about yourself. It requires you to have integrity, to walk the talk and lead by example. It requires communicating directly, not through others, and seeking to understand

the reasons why people do what they do. Cultivating trusting relationships is seen as naïve for cynical old political animals, but it is fundamental to creating change that matters and change that lasts.

Suspend your judgment

Human beings are quick to judge. It takes us about seven seconds to make a judgment when we meet a new person. This was very important when we lived in caves and we had to work out pretty quickly whether the creature at the front door was going to eat us or not. Having a finely tuned instinct for people is a great thing and it's what we teach kids at school about stranger danger. But it's when that lingers as judgment that it gets unfair and a bit nasty. We do it all the time. The dad in the supermarket who yells at his kids is a bad parent. But hey, maybe he's raising the kids on his own and he worked a late shift and he's worn out, like we all are sometimes. Teen parents pushing a pram through the mall have ruined their lives. But maybe they adore their baby and are doing an awesome job. Ask anyone who has experienced homelessness and poverty and they'll tell you it's the looks people give them that's the hardest thing to deal with. It's the stigma. And that's not even a real thing; it's just a construct in our heads and it's easily changed.

When you label someone you stop listening to them.

HELLO
MY NAME IS

How many times have you judged someone by their behaviour and then found out something about them that makes you feel bad that you judged them? Maybe you gave them a label or went along with the label others gave them. 'Crazy Heidi' and her mad ideas from the first chapter, who turned out to be a passionate idealist trying to change the world. When you label someone you stop listening to them. You close yourself off to the complexities of their human-ness and you stop trying to understand them. In the tribal realm of party politics, labels are just how things are. It's a short cut for understanding. They're a Tory, a Lib, a greenie, a leftie, a redneck. And with those labels comes a whole load of assumptions about the other person. This may have been fine in much simpler times when we all voted the way our fathers had. But the world is more complex; the positions we take are more nuanced.

We need to understand those nuances if we are to find common ground and get solutions. Of course we can't always have endless, in-depth conversations to try to understand where people are coming from – that takes way too long – and it would be a bit weird and intense anyway. But there are clues everywhere if we pay attention. We can have a greater understanding of people's values and motivations when we really listen to what they're saying, how they say it and what they do.

Amanda is from a family of wealthy businesspeople. She loves business and has made millions in property development. Money gives her the freedom to spend time with her daughters. She says anyone who slaves away for other people as an employee is stupid – they are wasting their lives. I found this out when I set myself the task of connecting with someone who was very different to me. Over coffee I asked Amanda about her story, her motivations and dreams, and I listened. Amanda was someone I would normally avoid or dismiss as being too shallow and self-interested. Before I went I made a note of all the judgments and assumptions I held about her, based on what I had read online. Surprise, surprise – when I suspended those judgments and actually listened, I discovered she was overcoming her own challenges and loved her family just like I did. In the Presencing Institute's Theory U training this is called an 'empathy walk', which is about spending time with people who are different to you and listening without judgment. New political animals need to get out of the echo chambers of people who agree with them and take an empathy walk every now and then.

Powerful conversation

Consider how our parliaments are designed – as inside versions of the traditional battlefield. In his book, *Recollections of a Bleeding Heart*, Don Watson refers to Elias Canetti, describing modern parliament as 'all that is left of the original lethal clash... it is played out in many forms, with threats, abuse and physical provocation which may lead to blows or missiles. But the counting of the vote ends the battle'.

Mainstream media is set up the same simplistic way, with 'sides' providing their responses to some false binary question. Social media has become a shouty version of the old model, where the words people tap out condemn them to that position for life. Our whole world can seem like a tennis match of accusation and blame. For old political animals it is all about the debate – I put my argument, you counter with your argument. The most important thing is to sound confident and look like you know what you're doing.

What would a more powerful conversation look like?

Think about the last time you were part of a really energising conversation, when you walked away feeling really alive.

How about the opposite? Can you think of a conversation that drained all your energy and made you feel flat?

What made the difference?

Training your political animal to have powerful conversations can help you move mountains.

Imagine a new politics that is all about having a dialogue with each other. To achieve this we need to bring our curiosity, like the Buddhist teaching about the dog and the lion. Throw a stick to a dog and it will chase the stick. Throw a stick to a lion and it will turn back to see what threw the stick. When we're curious we wonder why people do what they do, why they make the choices they make, why they said that thing or did that thing. Next time you read a story in the media about a document that has been leaked, don't get drawn into the content of the document, ask yourself – who leaked it and why would they do that?

In a powerful conversation we ask genuine questions rather than become defensive and try to convince the other side that they're wrong.

In a powerful conversation we ask genuine questions rather than become defensive and try to convince the other side that they're wrong. We try to understand why a person has that point of view. What is the motivation behind the comment?

Otto Scharmer of the Presencing Institute describes it as 'having a jacket, not being my jacket'. When I debate I am my jacket. The position I hold is so bound up in my identity that when you attack my comment you are attacking me, and I duly get defensive. When we instead engage in dialogue, I am wearing a jacket but it's not all of me; I can take it off. So when you have a different point of view to mine I see it just as a different point of view and I am curious about that.

The shift political animals need to make is away from finding the 'right answer' to finding the 'right question' – that is a question that helps the person have an insight. For example, when the kids get home from school, instead of asking, 'What did you do today?' ask, 'What made you laugh today?' In this question, rather than asking them to recall the facts as they played out, you're asking them to reflect on their experience and the insights they had. We can train our political animals to hold conversations that take people out of their own bubble and see reality with different eyes. This can lead them to build more meaningful relationships, generate new ideas and create a profound shift in mindset.

PRACTICE TIPS

We are braver when we have friends standing alongside us. We can challenge accepted truths without feeling so vulnerable and without fear of being cast out of the tribe. Building meaningful relationships is the foundation of political work and it must be more purposeful than accidental. New political animals must move beyond the transactional behaviour of the old politics in order to make change that matters and lasts. To find allies and hold onto them, political animals

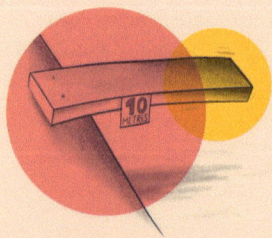

need to treat trust as a gift that's handed out freely. They need to notice when they are judging and labelling others and break that habit by being curious and listening, like I did with wealthy property developer Amanda. Asking powerful questions that help others have insights into themselves and the world around them will leave you with friends for life.

Reliable friends

A measure of resilience is when you have at least one person you can go to if you need help.
Who is that person for you? If you decided to challenge an accepted truth, who would stand with you?

The gift of trust

Trust is generally hard won and easily lost.
When has someone done something that caused you to lose trust in them? What would you need to let go of to mend that broken trust?

Take an 'empathy walk'

Seek out someone who is quite different to you, who may disagree with you, perhaps from a different social class, with different values or beliefs. Sit with them for a while, ask open questions and be curious about their perspective (don't get defensive). Maybe make a note of your assumptions beforehand so you can notice what's changed after the conversation.

Ask powerful questions

During the early days of the pandemic, when employees were working from home, managers asked different sorts of questions. They asked, 'What is causing you stress right now? What is the source of your hope?'

Other powerful questions are:

What keeps you awake at night?

What has inspired you lately?

What moves you to tears?

What do you love doing? How did you come to love it?

Try spending a day asking questions instead of making statements. Make sure they are open questions, that is, questions that don't have simple 'yes/no' answers, and help the other person have insights about themselves or their situation.

Chapter 5:
Know your target

Know the enemy and know yourself; in a hundred battles you will never be in peril. When you are ignorant of the enemy, but know yourself, your chances of winning or losing are equal. If ignorant both of your enemy and yourself, you are certain in every battle to be in peril.

– SUN TZU

Lobbyists charge exorbitant fees to crawl through the halls of power, using every bit of knowledge they've gathered about a decision-maker in order to influence them. They know their target's weak spots, pressure points, and ways into a negotiation to get their client the result they want. We now know that the online influencing of voters is a multimillion-dollar and very powerful business that can change the outcome of elections. It's not surprising, then, that when we talk about influencing decision-makers it can conjure up images of smarmy, shallow operators in shiny suits. To many purists this is another form of manipulation, and they would rather win the day with coherent argument than cultivate a false relationship. Sure, that would be great. And we may live in that sort of world one day, when decision-makers are absolutely, resolutely focused on doing the right thing above all else. But right now we have to assume there's a lot more than the facts going into the making of the decision.

So if you don't make an effort to get to know your target, then you will lose the argument. And you'll miss the opportunity to change the perspective of the decision-maker. The fundamental difference for new political animals is that they're finding points of connection so they can build the bridge together, not out of self-interest but for the common good.

No one loves your idea as much as you do

It's great that you're passionate about your idea. It really is. But it's highly unlikely that the person who holds the key to whether your idea happens is on the same page as you. They've got a lot on, a million competing priorities, and a bottom drawer full of other people's good ideas. That means you need to persuade them. And the best way to do that is to let go of your ideals and think about your issue from their point of view. This is the art of influencing, and it requires a deep understanding of your target.

A health academic called Reshma had failed to persuade a health minister to fund a strategic project on obesity that focused on the social determinants of health. Feeling very frustrated, she could not understand why the compelling research she and her colleagues presented just did not cut through. She had taken an assumption with her to the crucial meeting: that the minister was a rational being who would make a decision based purely on evidence and logic. Reshma is, of course, a highly intelligent person, but it was her political intelligence that was lacking in this instance.

She failed to get in the shoes of the decision-maker and see the issue from his point of view.

Ask a question like, 'What needs to change for you to fund a proposal like this?'

If Reshma and her colleagues had spent some time gathering intel before the meeting they could have taken a different approach. They could have considered the different narratives going on in the minister's head. He was thinking about the political pressure he was facing over emergency department waiting times, about his ambition to be the leader, about the election that was one year away and his need for ideas he could sell to the electorate. Reshma could have reframed her proposal into a document that had political benefits, with arguments the minister could use to convince his colleagues to spend the money. Time spent with government ministers, CEOs and leaders of all kinds is gold. Use it to understand their motivations and test your own assumptions, so you can give your idea the best chance of success. Use the opportunity ask a question like, 'What needs to change for you to fund a proposal like this?'

They may never love your idea as much as you do, but they may see a reason to support it. It's up to you as the political animal to deeply understand those reasons, the risks and the benefits, and create a connection with your target that benefits the people you are making the change for. This is the powerful art of influencing.

The powerful art of influencing

In my utopia, leaders make their decisions based on vision, reasoned argument and evidence. They push aside those who yell the loudest and listen for the quiet voices. They have a strong sense of what's right and the personal courage to stand up for justice. We're not there yet. We're going to have to play the game for a bit longer so we can change the game.

Sophie called me late one night in a panic because an Australian Senator was visiting her community centre the next day. It was the middle of an election campaign and the centre's staff were desperate for funds to keep their community store going. She ran her pitch past me. She'd done meticulous research and was preparing to ask the Senator which bucket of funding would be best for them to apply for, and would he please support their application. I pulled her up there.

I said, 'How about you be him: a politician in the middle of an election campaign. What is at the front of his mind right now?'

'Winning the election?' she asked, tentatively.

'Correct', I said. 'So as he walks into your centre there are only two things he is listening for: what will make him look good and what could make him look bad. Your job is to help him see that giving you the funding you need will make him look good in your community and then people are more likely to vote for him and his party. If he doesn't give you the funding, that will do his reputation no good at all.'

I left her with homework on how many people use the centre and the numbers of people connected to them –

basically, how many votes the staff at that community centre can influence.

This is an example of a transactional conversation. In the middle of a high-pressure situation like an election campaign, it's about all you can hope for. Your real power comes when you can give that decision-maker a meaningful experience that nudges their world view in the direction of common good for long-term change.

Jill was the CEO of a not-for-profit mental health organisation. The responsible government minister was a neo-liberal who believed individuals are responsible for their own health – the only role government needs to play is running hospitals, not engaging in preventative health programs. Jill and her colleagues had many frustrating attempts at lobbying for funding and policy change. One day she decided to do something different. She took along to the meeting a person the minister knew, the son of a well-known resident of his electorate.

The young man had contracted diabetes and was struggling psychologically with the impact it was having on his life. He was on stress leave from his job and was taking anti-depressants. He quietly shared his story and the minister listened. The minister was moved enough to investigate the lack of psychology services for people with diabetes. Jill got a result for her organisation and her clients. She also influenced the intransigent minister, changing his view of the world ever so slightly.

Jill had done her thinking on what would influence her target, and she had used her circle of influence, finding someone else in her network to deliver the message.

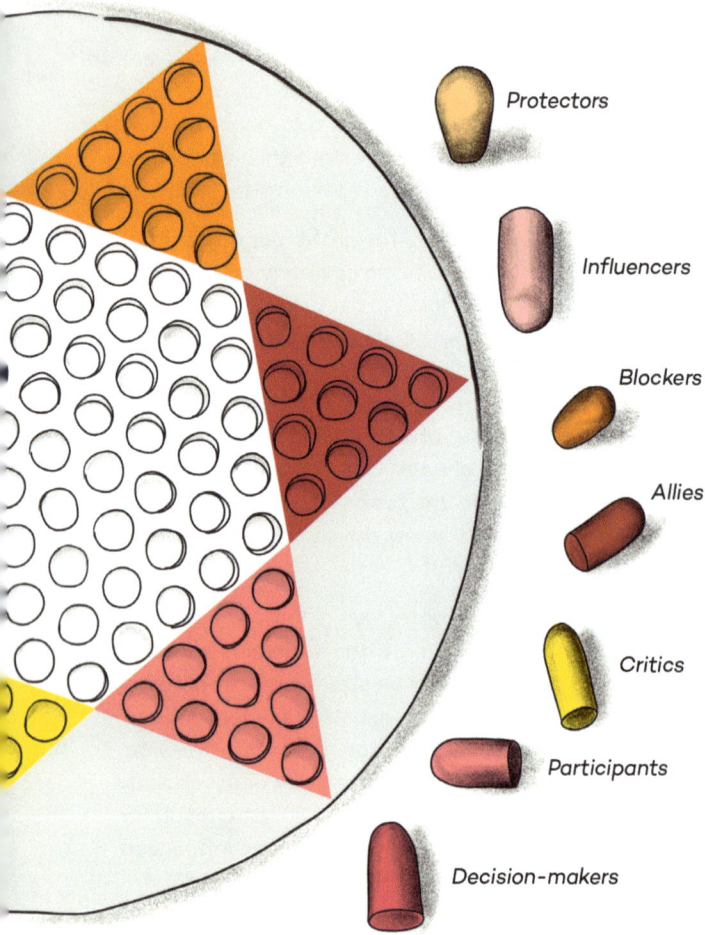

Protectors

Influencers

Blockers

Allies

Critics

Participants

Decision-makers

Your circle of influence

When you set out to change your world, the most powerful resource you have is your relationships. We tend to stumble through life making chance connections with people, and it's only when we need help that we see how far, or not, our network reaches. Political animals need to be smart about who is in their network. To make change for good you need to build your political capital and take a strategic approach to your relationships, reaching out to people who can help your cause, as well as those who may get in your way. 'Know your enemy', as Sun Tzu said, and a whole load of other people on the way through. So who is in your circle of influence, and who is outside your circle that you need to bring in?

Let's think about them as different types: your protector, decision-makers, influencers, participants, allies, critics and blockers.

Protector

We already know that stepping out alone to challenge accepted truths is not easy. What helps is if you have a protector. A protector is someone who is in a more powerful position than you — they have status or networks that are stronger than yours. Think about a time in your life when someone has had your back, whether it was at work, at school, in sport. You can go and do what you need to because someone else is looking out for you. If you are criticised they'll defend you and if you need help they'll stand with you. The situation you may be more familiar with is when no one has your back. This can be pretty scary, and you may not realise you're so vulnerable until something goes wrong and there's no one beside you. **Without a protector you're more likely to just turn up and keep your head down, or you may walk away altogether.**

Decision-makers

We are all decision-makers, but in this context we are focusing our attention on the one person who holds the power to make the decision that's important to us. When it comes to taking action on the change you want to see, you don't always need to convince everyone. You can often target your effort to the one person who makes the ultimate decision. It may be the head of your team or the boss of your organisation. It could be the chair of the board, but it may not be; sometimes there are people around who don't have the title but they do have some power. **It's really valuable to find out how the decision-maker got into the position they hold now and who keeps them there.**

Influencers

In our complex world, decision-makers rarely make important decisions on their own; they'll seek out the advice of others. These influencers may carry their own power because of their position, or the relationships they have. In communities we call them the 'town talkers'. You probably know who I'm talking about at work, in your group or community. Imagine the person who runs the local post office. They seem to know everyone, but they don't always know the power they have. **If the influencers like you and your idea they are a fantastic asset, but if they're not on your side you're in strife.**

Participants

If you are making change that has an impact on the lives of others, then the most important people to have in your network are the ones who will be impacted by that change. The participants should be at the centre of your circle. If you've had a great idea to fix a problem in someone's life but you haven't asked them, you'd better. If you are designing a new staff room at the factory, ask the staff who will use it. If you are developing a healthy lunchbox program at school, ask the kids (and the parents). **Making sure the participants are at the centre is the foundation of the field of design thinking, and it represents a fundamental change in thinking that plays out as a shift in power from 'we know best' to 'they know best'.**

Allies

Your allies or supporters are the friends you can rely on. You can call on them to help you, for money and advice. They'll defend you and will stand with you when you're going through the tough times. **The more allies you have the stronger your relational power, and these numbers matter when you are trying to influence decision-makers.** There are more tips on getting the numbers in Chapter 6.

Critics

It is tempting to call your critics your enemies, but that sets up a dichotomy drawn from the old politics. Knowing who your critics are, and what they say about you and your idea, is important. But what's more important is understanding their motivation, where they're coming from, and then engaging with them. Can they be changed or do you need to work around them? Keep communication lines open with them, know what their criticisms are and be ready with responses. As sceptics, your critics are really useful, they will find the holes in your strategy, so go and talk to them when you're ready. Living as we do in our bubbles of like-minded people, we may not have others with vastly different points of view in our circle. **Also, it's hard to hear criticism without getting defensive and so we have a natural desire to move away from them.** Instead, seek them out, listen to what they have to say and move towards them, not away. As Abraham Lincoln said, 'Do I not destroy my enemies when I make them my friends?'

They'll point out rules and processes and precedents and consequences in a world where all roads lead to 'No'.

Blockers

Blockers are basically human-shaped brick walls. They're not as open as critics; they won't always tell you they don't like your idea; they'll just quietly place themselves in your way. They'll point out rules and processes and precedents and consequences in a world where all roads lead to 'No'. Unlike criticism that can be informative, the blockers' subversion and undermining is just annoying. Understand your blockers – what motivates them and what they're afraid of. It's highly likely that they benefit from the status quo and feel they stand to lose something from the change you're proposing, such as control, status or money. There may be ways to work with them, but often you will need to go around them.

The most challenging circumstance is when the decision-maker is also a blocker. It will take some crafty alliance-building, influencing skills and patience to get around them.

Have a look at the section in this chapter on 'dealing with the blockers'.

Avoid the spray and pray

If you want to change a process at work, get a new project up, or change a law, you may not need to convince everyone, just the people who make the decision. The spray-and-pray method takes a lot of time, energy and resources that you may not have. So set aside your plans for a broad community campaign and put your effort into really understanding your target. Who do you need to influence to achieve your outcome?

When people feel passionate about an issue it's exciting to come together as a group and organise a campaign. This is what happened when the government made changes to arts policy that reduced funding and downgraded its importance. Some local artists were angry and they got together to organise a campaign. Being creatives, they first came up with a fantastic design concept, a punchy slogan and clever logo. They were ready to activate their networks and launch a photo campaign on social media with their slogan, but what was missing was a clear objective. What outcome did they want? The decision reversed, more funding, better policy? Once they answered that question they realised they could better target their effort and keep the campaign idea in the back pocket as a Plan B. A broad campaign can be useful to 'scare the bear' (as the Canadians would say) through the power of numbers, but you might be better off firing an arrow that hits your target between the eyes.

When I was a political adviser in the early 2000s we were trying to change the law to give equal rights to people in same-sex relationships. It was an issue whose time had come well and truly – it was the right thing to do. Our law reform proposal generated a lot of opposition among some members of the community who had considerable influence over certain members of parliament. To make sure we were successful in getting the legislation passed we had to focus our effort.

The first task in our strategy was to work out who the ultimate decision-makers were. They weren't the general public, so we didn't need to run a campaign through the media. They weren't the vocal critics either, so we had to make sure we didn't let ourselves get distracted by a noisy minority. We tasked one staff member with managing the critics and the media, and we put the bulk of our effort into convincing five members of the parliament's upper house – three of whom would hold the votes we needed. We worked out what and who would have the best chance of persuading them to support this reform. We crafted arguments to address their concerns. We introduced them to individuals from their own electorates who had persuasive stories to tell. We stayed focused on our target and the law passed with the support of the three members we needed.

Who do you think you're talking to?

Before you write that proposal, before you walk into that meeting, before you make that phone call, stop and think about who you're talking to.

What do you know about the decision-maker, this human on which your idea (and the future of the planet) depends? Before you write that proposal, before you walk into that meeting, before you make that phone call, stop and think about who you're talking to.

We know that it's probably unlikely that this person will see things the same way you do. Reacquaint yourself with the three centres we talked about in Chapter 3 (head, heart and body). If you walk in with a head full of concepts, spewing theories and quoting lofty academics, and the person you're trying to influence makes decisions from the heart centre, they won't even hear you. You'll be like an alien jabbering on, making a noise while their eyes glaze over and they start to think about lunch. If you walk in pushing for action and are scant on detail and the decision-maker operates from the head centre, then you're at risk of freaking them out completely. It's really important to work out what they are listening and looking for in your pitch.

To give you an example, this is the sort of checklist a government minister runs through when they're listening to your idea and making a decision (in roughly this order):

- ✓ Will I get the support of my faction (at a bare minimum, will I alienate anyone important in my faction)?

- ✓ Will I get cabinet support?

- ✓ Will I get caucus support?

- ✓ Will it make me look good?

- ✓ Will I be criticised in the media?

- ✓ Will my constituents still vote for me? Could it cost me my seat?

- ✓ Is there enough money in the budget?

- ✓ Will I get other groups offside?

- ✓ Will it blow over before the election?

- ✓ Is it the right thing to do?

Maybe this is too cynical. Some politicians are more emotionally intelligent and have the strength of character to do what is right ahead of what serves their self-interest, but the other considerations still play a part in their decision-making.

It's impossible to know what's going through the mind of a decision-maker. At work you might do all the preparation in the world and then lose it all because your boss is having a bad day. Influencing is hard to do, but if we want to change our world, political animals need to get better at it. You may only need to be just a bit better at it than the next person to contribute to a great decision for the greater good.

When you're sizing up your target you can spend a few minutes thinking about how to pitch to them or you can prepare a whole strategy. Even if you haven't met them before, there are clues. What can you assume about them based on what's on the public record? What do others say about them? Can you work out from what they say and do whether they operate more from their head, heart or body centre? What clues are around to tell you how they consume information? Some people like words and time to think. Some are highly visual and want information presented a certain way, like in video. Others are highly numerate and love the data, so they need spreadsheets, graphs and diagrams. And some respond best to stories, so come armed with personal anecdotes.

In a workshop a group of community advocates was trying to work out how to persuade the local council to fund a program that builds relationships between police and young people. They worked out it was the council's general manager they had to convince. Being a small town, there were people in the room who knew a bit about him, and someone said, 'I reckon he's a stats man'. It's always a good idea to check assumptions, so the council's annual report was pulled up on screen and they scrolled through the general manager's report. He was definitely into statistics. So they crafted their pitch using the relevant data, making nice charts and tying their proposal to the strategic goals of the council. Their proposal was well-received and got them to first base.

Dealing with the blockers

Coming up against people who get in the way of your positive change can be frustrating and exhausting. It happens all the time. No doubt you've heard many versions of 'No', like the classic, 'We've tried it before and it didn't work'. But before you jump headlong into a confrontation with the blockers, consider first what your own motivations are and what their motivations are, then you can decide whether you can work with them or you have to work around them – or go through them.

A political animal and social justice advocate called Tori is one of those rare humans who doesn't mind conflict. She would do whatever it took to get good outcomes for her constituents, and if that required direct confrontation with a blocker, then so be it. She would hold her ideas and views tightly, defending them to the death. Over time she came to realise that challenging people in positions of power wasn't always the best strategy, and in fact it was damaging her relationships and her reputation. She needed to listen and understand.

Blockers often benefit from the situation being the way it is and have no desire to upend the status quo.

To work with blockers, political animals need to get in the blockers' shoes. Blockers often benefit from the situation being the way it is and have no desire to upend the status quo. They may be afraid of change, so find out what they fear. Do they see a risk to their reputation, status or relationships? See your interactions as an opportunity to help allay their fears and build their confidence that things will work out. Try to find out how they see your situation. What do you agree on and connect on?

Some blockers are just hard work and you have to go around them.

Ideally, over time you will build authentic relationships with them that are based on a mutual respect. While you may never be besties, the least you can hope for is that you've built your political capital enough so that, as old political animals say, 'When they come for you, they'll come at you from the front not the back' (apologies for the knife-wielding metaphor). Some blockers are just hard work and you have to go around them.

This can take time and you may just have to commit yourself to playing the long game (as we see in Chapter 7). Tori had to employ all her political animal tactics when dealing with a government minister who was blocking a policy change she was trying to achieve for refugee women. In a meeting with the minister Tori found out which committee he was getting his advice from about this particular piece of policy. Because she had spent years building strategic relationships, Tori knew many people who were active on the issue, including a member of the committee. She knew she had to influence the advice that was going to the minister, so she approached the committee member.

The committee member wasn't convinced she would get the support of her colleagues, so she and Tori prepared a proposal to conduct a targeted consultation process with relevant organisations. The committee

agreed and organisations were given opportunities in forums to present their views on the policy change. Their views were written into the committee's report, ultimately changing the advice that went to the minister and taking Tori and her allies a step closer to achieving the policy change they wanted. As a new political animal, Tori had no need to be attached to the policy and this lack of ego enabled her to work behind the scenes to get the best outcome for refugee women and their children.

A direct challenge to a government minister who is both a blocker and the decision-maker is a risky tactic. Tori could have organised her allies to lobby for change through the media, start a petition, march in the streets or use a range of other public tactics. In some circumstances this may have been appropriate. And necessary. But by going behind the scenes and using a process that the minister himself set up, Tori was able to maintain a relationship that will continue to be valuable into the future.

The same applies in the workplace. When the blocker of the change you are trying to make is your boss, you need to get crafty. Unless you are prepared for a direct confrontation, or to quit your job, you probably need to stay on good terms. So be strategic, build up your relational power with others in your organisation. Try reframing your idea to meet the needs of the organisation and its leaders. Stay open – it is just possible that your blocker can transform into an ally when you build trust with them.

Remember, we don't always agree with each other and we don't have to, but people with different views can come together to make good decisions for the benefit of others.

When you've tried working *with* a blocker, and then going *around* them, but they're still intransigent, you'll need to go *through* them. This may happen in a public way, or it may happen in a private situation like a meeting. You may need to name up some issues and ('with all due respect') speak truth to power. But be careful, direct confrontation can easily draw fire and brimstone in return, and when your combatant feels humiliated they are far less likely to give your cause an easy passage.

When you find yourself in this situation don't forget to engage your emotional intelligence. Ask yourself what your own motivation is for confronting the blocker. If it's your pride, your desperate need to be right or to have the last word, then go drop your ego off at the door. Stay focused on your long-term goals and the people who will benefit from your actions.

Present a different perspective on the issue – help the blocker understand the issue from another viewpoint.

Remember, we don't always agree with each other and we don't have to, but people with different views can come together to make good decisions for the benefit of others. To find common ground you may need to be prepared to give up the perfect for the good – for now.

Make your pitch

Now that you're clear on who your target is and where they're coming from, it's time to make your pitch. Whether it's written down or a conversation or both, you've got to start with a positive. For bosses and leaders it's a real bummer to be smacked over the head with everything that is wrong, especially in these uncertain times when we seem to be swamped with new problems every day. Again, put yourself in their shoes – would you want to have to bathe in someone else's criticism of you? Rather than shout about what's not working, start by giving attention to what is working and the good things that are being done to solve the problem. Instead of saying, 'Youth unemployment in our region has risen to 25 per cent and our young people are at risk of never having a job', say, 'The (such and such) program to connect young people to employers is working and we need to build on that'. If you can't find something that *is* working, then talk about the opportunity.

Decision-makers are busy people and do not have time for you to get to your point. If you're writing a pitch, don't craft a mystery novel with a big reveal at the end. Put the most important information at the beginning. And don't think you need to use big, fancy words to sound smart. Your reader will appreciate it when you are concise, make your case efficiently, and are clear in what you're asking for.

Here's a structure that works for conversations and written pitches. If it's a longer document then summarise these three points in a sentence or two at the beginning before you go into your detail.

1. Open with vision. Be inspiring about your hope for the future. Paint a picture with words of what it looks like and feels like. Use the language of values to connect with your listener or reader, like community and fairness. Talk about what's working, what the existing strengths are, and congratulate or thank them if you can.

2. Set out the barriers and challenges. Outline what's not working and what's getting in the way of achieving that future. Be specific about the barriers that are within the decision-maker's control. Outline the risks if change doesn't happen. Use data and stories to make your argument.

3. Present the solutions. Show the listener or reader how they can overcome the barriers. Make them real and achievable. If you want something specific, then don't forget to ask. Whether it's money, advice, support or something else you need, be direct and make it clear.

One common way of thinking about pitching is to imagine you have 30 seconds in an elevator with the decision-maker. How would you get your message across? This is a common technique, often used to help people hone their message, but it doesn't ever actually happen, right? Well it did happen to our political animal, Tori.

Tori's organisation had been trying for weeks to get a meeting with the state's premier to talk about a bill that was being tabled in parliament. Their calls were not being returned and the day before the legislation was due, they got desperate. In a last-ditch effort to secure an outcome, Tori grabbed

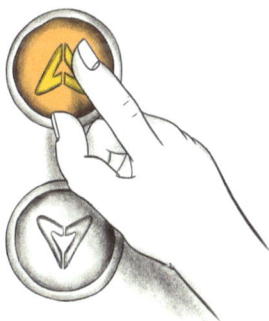

the important paperwork and took off to the premier's office. It was in the days before mandatory security passes, and Tori decided the best course of action was to ride the elevator. The premier finally entered with his adviser on his way to Parliament House. Tori spread the document out on the wall, pointed to the key paragraph and said, 'We need this or the deal is off'. The Premier looked at her, probably shocked by her audacity, and turned to his adviser and said, 'Give them what they want'.

This is a brazen example of the 30-second elevator pitch, and it came at the end of many weeks of negotiations. It shows that you can be as strategic as you like, but sometimes you need to be sure of your message then seize your opportunities with a bit of courage and good timing.

PRACTICE TIPS

If you don't know who you need to convince, you can waste a lot of time and energy. You'll give your idea the best chance of success if you get in the decision-maker's shoes, like not-for-profit CEO Jill and Sophie from the community centre learned. This is where political animals need to be pragmatic because if you don't play the game, others will, and they won't always be motivated by the common good. So know who's in your circle of influence and understand how the power flows. Spend time investigating your target – find out what makes them tick and what they are listening for when you're talking

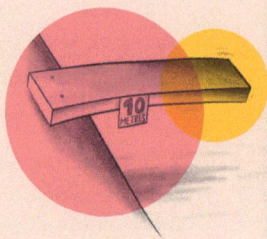

to them. Every interaction is a precious opportunity to nudge others ever so slightly in the direction of making better decisions and creating a better world.

Who's in your circle?

When you're thinking about making change or challenging accepted truths, who's got your back? Who will stick up for you when others are speaking against you? Who are your critics and blockers of the change you're trying to make? Is there a clear decision-maker that you can target your effort towards? Who influences them? And, most importantly, who is the change for? All of these relationships matter, so understand them and think about what you need from them.

Get in their shoes

What is the decision-maker looking for? What are they listening for? What are the risks for them in what you're proposing? What are the benefits? What do you need to say and do to influence them? You can spend five minutes thinking about where they're coming from or you can prepare a whole strategy.

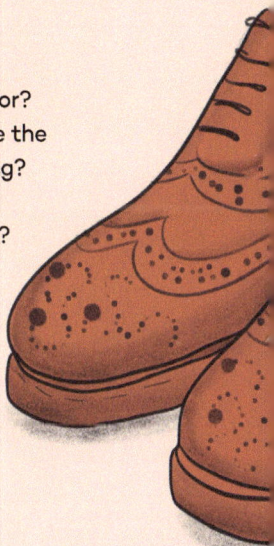

Prepare your pitch

Make the most out of your opportunity to pitch an idea by using a simple structure like this:

1. Open with your vision for a better future, the opportunities and existing strengths.

2. Set out the challenges you're experiencing and the barriers to achieving that vision.

3. Hand over the solutions that will overcome the barriers and build on the strengths.

What does this look like in one sentence as a 30-second pitch?

Chapter 6: Organise

We can do this together, because while individually you have purpose, together we have power.

– STACEY ABRAMS

What about when the change you're trying to make is much bigger than you?
Maybe you don't just want to influence the decision-maker, you want to *become* the decision-maker. Perhaps something goes wrong and you find yourself suddenly in a leadership role that you didn't plan for. Others are looking to you, at work or in your community, to challenge the way things are done, to change the system. Our personal resources can only take us so far. To do the big stuff, political animals need to be able to harness the power of the group. They need to organise. In this chapter we make the transition from personal power ('power within') into collective power ('power with').

Pulling a group of people together comes with a word of warning: this is precisely the moment when everything can fall apart. You might come together, for example, around your common desire for a new

bike path through your town, but that purpose won't hold you for long. It would be lovely (but perhaps a little dull) if human beings all somehow magically got along, but the old politics shows us that once the polite chat moves through, the egos, self-interest and power plays take over. Before you know it, the original group has split into factions and the agenda becomes about slashing the tyres on the bikes of the other faction rather than lobbying for bike paths that everyone can enjoy. It doesn't have to be this way. There's plenty that political animals can do to hold a group together so they can achieve their goal, make a difference, and empower others along the way.

Organising, or community organising as it is also called, is a framework for taking action on social justice by building collective power. This is what American politician Stacey Abrams did so successfully in Georgia in the 2020 United States elections: her organisation, Fair Fight, registered 800,000 people to vote for the first time in their lives. In this chapter we draw some lessons from that organising framework, but there are much better resources elsewhere for those political animals who want to go deeper.

The angry mob

Have you ever been to a protest rally? What motivated you to go? Frustration and anger? To be with like-minded people? To feel connected, empowered, and add to the strength of numbers? Perhaps you saw it as something that was easy to do – turn up for a few hours for a cause. These are some of the answers I get when I ask this question in workshops. Others say they want to be a role model for their children and show them that it's important to care enough to show up.

It's actually a big deal to place yourself in an environment of dissent, to make demands, challenge accepted truths, and question the authority of the leaders.

It's a human right, of course – freedom of peaceful assembly and association – and some of us in healthy democracies may take this for granted. But it's actually a big deal to place yourself in an environment of dissent, to make demands, challenge accepted truths, and question the authority of the leaders.

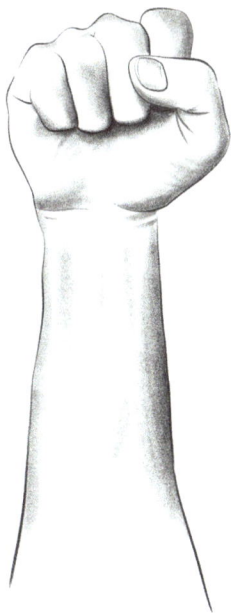

You give your time, effort and emotions to being part of the angry mob. In times of crisis, putting your body in a physical space with others is an incredibly powerful act. It can be such an empowering experience.

And so it feels a bit mean to ask the follow-up question: what changed as a result of the rally? This is where the workshop participants turn a bit sad and their cynicism bubbles to the surface. Some say nothing changed as a result of the rally. Others say things did change but it took a few more years to happen, or that something changed but not what they wanted or how they wanted. Where did all that passion and energy go? How can it all just dissipate into the beige of business as usual? Well it does happen, more often than we realise, and there's a key reason for that: the angry mob has passion for change but they're not organised.

After revolutions it's not typically the protest leaders and participants who immediately take power, it's an already-existing organisation, a political party or an army. Think about the protesters storming the US Capitol in January 2021; the story would have been devastatingly different if they'd been organised and connected to a formal institutional power like the military.

The lesson from history is that as individuals we may be motivated to make change, but it's not enough. It's easy for each of us to click on a petition, or complain in the corridors, or even to march in the street, but to make significant change we need to be able to hold a disparate group of human beings together and build their power. Of course, you may not want to stage a coup and take over parliament, but you may want to tackle the bullying culture on your board, or bring the practices of your local progress association into the 21st century, or take staff concerns about workplace safety to your belligerent boss. **To do those things, you need to know where the power lies.**

Do a power map

Raoul was appointed to a management position in an insurance agency. He was moving across from a less senior position in another department and lacked some of the content knowledge, but the recruitment panel decided it wouldn't take him long to step up to the role. Raoul is an introvert — he's good at strategy and analysis, but he's not a people person. He works hard and doesn't have time to stop and chat with staff. It wasn't long before he found himself out of the loop on some key areas of work. Other senior managers seemed to know more than he did. One in particular, the finance manager, Gail, seemed to be the 'go to' person in the organisation.

Gail was the sort of person who knew who got engaged on the weekend, who was applying for jobs in other areas, and who was on leave and why. She organised drinks on Friday nights and everyone seemed to love Gail. Without Gail on his side, Raoul was going to have a very hard time indeed. While he held the *positional power*, being the manager, Gail also had a lot of power. Not only did she run the finances, giving her the *money power*, she had also built up significant *relational power*. When Raoul leaves the organisation one day his replacement will assume the same positional power, but relational power is something everyone can work on at any time. Political animals need to not just rely on their positional power, if they have it, they also have to cultivate trusting relationships to get things done.

Being a political animal means you need to run the ultraviolet light over the invisible trail and find out where the real power lies.

We talked in Chapter 1 about power being invisible. You may only know it's there when you bump up against one of those human-shaped brick walls and find out there's a whole army behind that one. Being a political animal means you need to run the ultraviolet light over the invisible trail and find out where the real power lies.

Do a map of the people in your group, network, team or whole organisation. Quite possibly it looks like a traditional hierarchy – boss at the top, second-in-charge next, and whoever is there at the next level down, then anyone else who is relevant – and pop yourself in wherever you fit. You've created a picture of the formal power structure. The person at the top, who makes the big decisions, is the highest authority and they may have the most power. But they may not. Now highlight who has relational power in your organisation. Who is well-networked? Who seems to know what's going on? What is their relationship to senior management? How influential are they?

You don't need to be an extrovert or a 'people person' to build your relational power. You can do it just by being someone who can be trusted. When you are discreet people will tell you things and it's this knowledge that gives you your power. Also remember that power is fluid and people come and go. So don't rely too heavily on one powerful person; they may move on. If you are planning on challenging some accepted truths and shaking things up a bit, you'll need to keep yourself safe by building up your relational power. This is where the numbers are important.

The numbers

For old political animals it's called 'getting the numbers'. For new political animals it's called 'building leadership capacity to achieve your common purpose'. Sure, getting the numbers sounds simpler, and it's certainly more catchy, but the difference is fundamental to how we need to do politics in our complex, uncertain world. Getting the numbers is a series of transactional exchanges, like handshakes in a chain of IOUs weaving through the corridors.

We find the best examples of this practice in political parties, where decisions, like who gets the highly coveted positions on parliamentary committees, are determined not by talent, but by horse-trading between the factions. Let's take a fictional politician we'll call Michael the MP. When he wants a certain position he'll call around his colleagues, calling in debts ('You owe me'), and making promises ('I'll support you on the next thing'). Michael the MP gets that position on the committee – and the accompanying pay rise – not because he's the best person for the job, but because he got the numbers.

To achieve real change you need to reach beyond [the people you naturally get along with] to those who are different to you and who may disagree with you.

Tallying up the numbers was common practice for Chris, our political animal from Chapter 2, who had spent her career advocating on social justice issues. She would do research on colleagues to work out who was most likely to align with her values and beliefs and agree with her positions on issues and solutions. It was natural behaviour for her to operate this way, until one day she realised that it wasn't the right thing to do if she actually wanted to make the best decision. Chris learned that if she was to achieve meaningful outcomes for people, she needed to let go of an old habit of thinking, 'Who's going to support me because I'm right?' She removed her ego from the picture and replaced it with the people who would benefit from change. When she did that, she opened herself up to other points of view, other beliefs and solutions, and she worked to find common ground. This is how a new political animal operates, creating deeper relationships and building collective leadership capacity to achieve a common purpose.

While it's comforting to align yourself with the people you naturally get along with, to achieve real change you need to reach beyond these people to those who are different to you and who may disagree with you.

Getting along to get things done

When you think about it, workplaces are basically places where strangers come together to get things done. Over time you get to know each other, chatting about your personal life, kids, pets and hobbies. That is, if you have time – often we're way too busy for informal chats. We might catch snippets of information around the coffee machine, but how much do we really know about who we're working with?

Think about when you've joined a new group, maybe a board or committee or team. You go to your first meeting and after quick introductions they get straight into the tasks, running through the action list, checking timeframes and working out who's doing what. Fair enough, there's a lot to do and everyone's time poor, so best to crack on with it. The trouble is, when you don't take the time to get to know each other, you're second-guessing. While your colleague is talking, you're wondering why they're taking that position, and because no one has taken the time to get to know each other, you're left filling in the gaps with assumptions.

As a member of a newly established committee, our political animal, Chris, brought into her first meeting a whole lot of assumptions about everyone else in the group. She'd met some of them, and knew very little about others, so she looked them all up online and was confident she knew where they were all coming from. The pressure was on to get results, so the group got busy. Chris found out pretty quickly that her assumptions were all wrong. The group took a long time to form because it did not begin with an open conversation about who they were and how they would be as a collective.

The most fundamental thing strangers need to understand about each other is why. Why are you here? What is your motivation for turning up?

When we focus solely on what we do and ignore who we are, we are setting ourselves up to create change that does not work and does not last. So we waste our effort. The most fundamental thing strangers need to understand about each other is *why*. Why are you here? What is your motivation for turning up? Nailing that early on means you're on your way to building trust.

You may think that creating a cohesive group requires everyone to be the same. In fact, the opposite is true. It is diversity that is key to any group that comes together to achieve meaningful change in organisations and communities.

You may think that creating a cohesive group requires everyone to be the same. In fact, the opposite is true. It is diversity that is key to any group that comes together to achieve meaningful change in organisations and communities. From her experience in a range of decision-making bodies, Chris learned that you can't achieve positive outcomes without airing conflicting views. She says it is only by having your assumptions and ideas challenged by people who come from different perspectives that you can really test solutions. Political animals need to make sure they don't get stuck with a bunch of people who agree with them or are similar to them. When you can draw on people with diverse life experiences and perspectives you will avoid being trapped in your bubble and open yourself up to a world of options. The best decisions are made when you can see the whole picture from different angles.

New political animals challenge accepted truths and that involves risk. To find the courage and the confidence to take risks to make the change you want to see, you need to have trust in the people around you. Political animals need to be able to show leadership by leaving their egos and self-interest and any other baggage at the door and bring people together around a common good. This requires conversations, not just about the work you are setting out to do, but also who you will be as you do that work. And it's not just about who you'll be as an individual, it's also who you will be together as a group. You need to pay attention to the culture of the group if you are to exercise your collective power.

Powerful together

You'll know your group needs to work on its culture when gaps appear between what people are thinking and what they actually say. These are called 'unspeakables' – imagine them as closed doors behind which no one knows what is going on. The closed doors leave you with only assumptions and those assumptions can build into dramas that are much bigger than they need to be. The closer the gap is between what is thought and what is said, the more trusting is your culture.

Here are three things every group needs to get beyond the 'to do' lists, to nurture a healthy culture and trusting relationships. When you achieve these things you'll make better decisions and be more powerful together.

1. **Sense of purpose** – understand why you are in the room. Hearing from each other about why each person has shown up in this moment gets to the heart of our individual motivation, why we do what we do. Without it we are left wondering why people say and do certain things. This leads to assumptions and judgments being made and this can quickly erode trust.

2. **Sense of direction** – have a clear view of where you want to get to. Agree on a desired future that articulates what you want to achieve for others, and the sort of group you want to be. Make it inspiring. But don't be too prescriptive about how you get there; be open to what comes up.

3. **Shared values** – find the values that connect you all. What do we all value? It may be family, respect, integrity. Set the rules for how you will live those values through your decisions, and call it out when people behave in ways that conflict with your values.

Use your power to get an outcome that benefits someone else — who is not like you, who you've never met, who may not be born yet.

For new political animals setting out to make change there's another fundamental question that needs to stay front of mind: who is the change for? Knowing the answer to that question will keep you and your group focused. Making sure that the people who benefit from the change are actually leading the change will give you an even better chance of success. A key shift from the old politics to the new is to place the people concerned at the centre of decision-making and to put into action the phrase, 'Nothing about us without us'. This is where we remember, and extend, our definition of politics: use your power to get an outcome that benefits someone else – *who is not like you, who you've never met, who may not be born yet.*

People at the centre

For a long time the practice for solving some of the big problems faced by communities was for experts to come together, thrash out the solutions and then go out to the towns and suburbs to implement them. The experts are well-meaning, intelligent people – service providers and policy-makers – motivated by doing good in the world. But they often ignore one very important step in solving the problems: actually asking the people who live there what they think.

The so-called experts might feel good riding in on their white horses, tossing handfuls of glittering new solutions from their packs to grateful hordes. But the real experts, the people who live there, are left bewildered, turning to each other to say, 'Did you ask for this?', 'No I didn't ask for this, did you ask for this?', 'Well it's not what I would have done, but I guess they're here now so we should get them a cup of tea.' People-centred (or human-centred or co-design) approaches are becoming more common now, as decision-makers realise that when you don't ask the people who will be impacted by the decisions, you can waste money and effort on solutions that don't work and don't last.

Jenny was just ticking a box when she agreed to set up a panel of members of the public to discuss local health issues. Engaging people with lived experience was a process she had to get done as part of the project plan. When it came time to hold the first meeting she was actually quite nervous – worried about what might happen and that she might not be able to control it. Local government officials who were running the project turned up in their suits to the local council chambers where the meeting was being held. The lived-experience group, some with mental health and disability challenges, took their seats around the formal meeting table behind individual microphones. Not surprisingly, some of the participants were too intimidated to speak during that session. The power imbalance was all too clear.

It wasn't long before they joined together and suggested to the officials, 'How about you come to us?'

As part of the project the participants received some training to help them contribute to the project. It wasn't long before they joined together and suggested to the officials, 'How about you come to us?' The meeting venue was shifted to a place less formal and more familiar to the community members. It was a profound change that injected some equity into the power dynamics.

Over time Jenny changed to a more relaxed style of dress, loosened her grip on control and became more

open to what the community members were telling her. Eventually they became her allies in a decision about installing a specialist medical facility at the local health centre. Other members of the public had been agitating strongly for it, despite the fact that the same facilities were available close by at another health centre. Once the lived-experience group had received information about budgets, and were asked what should drop off the list in order to pay for the specialist facility, they decided it was not a priority and conveyed their views to the rest of the community.

There are plenty of people implementing change in communities, like developers, governments and councils, who run the standard tick-a-box consultations. They put out a paper, ask a few questions and say they've done extensive community engagement. It's all tightly controlled but not really genuine. For real change to happen, the engagement needs to be authentic and open. This first requires an acknowledgment of the power imbalance between the agency and the community, and for corrective measures to be put in place, like Jenny did. Then you have a sharing of power between those with the position and the money, and those with the lived experience. To achieve this balance, the decision-makers need to let go of their fears, assumptions and stereotypes, and learn to share.

Learn to share

There are a few reasons why decision-makers are afraid to share power with members of the community. They like to have a sense of control and worry that if they open up conversations, they won't be able to close them again. Hence the saying in the old politics, 'Don't ask a question that you don't know the answer to'. They are also afraid of not having the answers, and they may hold stereotypes about community members being unreasonable or overly emotional. In some cases this is justified; when people have been disenfranchised and ignored in the decisions that impact them they tend to get a bit angry. But what the organisers of processes like citizens' juries will tell you is that, when given the facts, human beings are pretty reasonable, and they are quite capable of making a decision that benefits the greater good.

Fear leads to control and that's where you see decision-makers holding tightly to their power. So while they might appear to want community input on a project, they may also be pushing a certain solution. This is what happened in a project Alex was working on about providing companionship for older people. The government agency was funding a model that gave one-on-one volunteer support to individuals. But when Alex asked older people in the community what they wanted, they preferred group models of companionship. That particular project was brought to an end by funding cuts, but the work continued as an informal befriending program. That's because the older people who participated organised themselves, used their power and created a model that worked for them. It turns out they didn't need a top-down model imposed on them, they just needed someone to start the conversation.

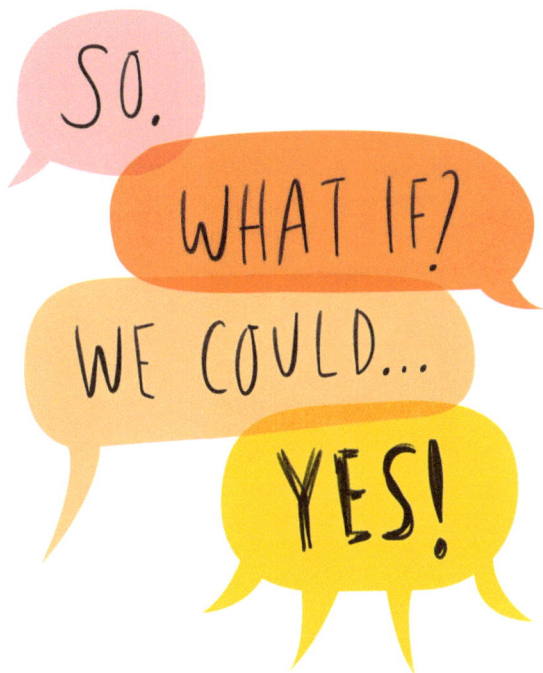

These older people had the confidence, skills and networks they needed to get their project going, but many people don't. New political animals need to create a space where people can develop the skills and confidence they need to work with others and take risks. This is especially important for people who are on the margins of society, living with poverty and discrimination, whose voices we rarely hear in decision-making.

When the people with the lived experience of a problem are supported by the people with the commitment to solve it, then real change can happen. For example, members of a community who want to stop a park being turned into a car park can come together, build their skills and become an effective lobby group. But it is when they have a few local councillors onside, who are prepared to stand up for their cause when the decision is being made, that their passion turns into power. Compass UK calls this '40° Change', when the people's grassroots informal power in civil society connects to the formal power held in institutions.

There is a risk when living in times of crisis that decision-makers will feel they have to act quickly, that there's no time to get a wide range of input into decisions. These are exactly the times we need to make sure people are empowered to make the decisions that affect their lives. The experience of coming together to solve problems is what builds connections and creates resilience for individuals, organisations and communities.

The political animals we need right now in these uncertain times are those who have learned to share power.

The political animals we need right now in these uncertain times are those who have learned to share power. They leave their egos at the door, knowing that it is enough that the job gets done, that a real difference is made. They don't need the medal, or the chest to pin it on. It's not about them, it's about the people they're doing it for and with. To gender-neutralise Lao Tsu's quote on leadership: A leader is best when people barely know they exist, when their work is done, their aim fulfilled, the people will say, we did it ourselves.

PRACTICE TIPS

Being passionate about your issue is nice, but it's not enough. To achieve meaningful change that lasts, you need to organise. That means you need to pull your allies together and hold them through a shared vision, sense of purpose and common values. When you take the time to understand each other, you will build trust and avoid the petty power plays that undo other well-meaning groups. Like Jenny and the lived-experience group, you create resilience in systems and communities when you share your power so that others can lead on the issues that impact them.

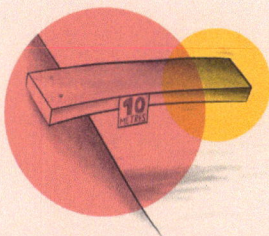

Map your power

Work out where power sits and how it moves through your group, organisation or community. Get out your sticky notes and write down names of key people. Place them on your map according to their formal power, according to their position or money. Now move them around according to their informal power, the relationships they have with others.

Who does the boss listen to when making decisions? Whose opinion matters? Who do you need to be

careful not to get offside? Who would you go to if you had a problem? Who do you need to talk to when you want to get something done? Who says jump and who asks, how high?

Where are you in this picture? What is the source of your power and how can you grow it? Who will you share it with so they too can grow?

Seek out diversity

When you get together as a group, check the perspectives of everyone in the room. As well as their motivation (their why), check age, race, gender, education and background. Then focus attention on whose perspectives are not in the room. It may be obvious that you have no people under 40 or no people of colour, or no people who really disagree with you.

Get out of your own bubble and seek out people who are different to you, even if it makes you uncomfortable.

Create a dynamic group

Take the time to get to know each other by asking questions that enable understanding and build trust. Try these:

How did you come to be part of this group? What quality do you bring?

What do you want to get out of this experience? What do you want to create through this experience?

As a group – what do we value most? How do we live our collective values every day?

How will we know when someone acts outside our values? What will we do if that happens?

Pay attention to who is speaking and who is not.

Who is leading and who is not? Be kind to yourself and each other. Being a new political animal is an organic process that is never complete. It's okay to stuff up, be vulnerable. Take time to reflect and evaluate. **Give each other constructive feedback and coach each other to create spaces where everyone is safe to step into their power.**

Articulate a deeper purpose

If you want to build a ship, don't drum up the men to gather wood, divide the work and give orders. Instead teach them to yearn for the vast endless sea.

– ANTOINE DE SAINT-EXUPERY

Political animals more easily connect with others when they have a clear sense of purpose. It's a deeper question that gets to the source of what motivates us, why we get out of bed each day and do what we do. Ask your group:

Why do we exist? What would happen if we didn't? And who would care?

Who do we do our work for, and with?

What is our highest possible potential as a group?

Let go of control

Be honest about your fears of opening up conversations to others. What is behind your need to control? What are you afraid of? What stereotypes do you hold onto?

Let them go and know that human beings, when given the opportunity, will be reasonable and make decisions that benefit the greater good.

Share your power

Be conscious of power imbalances and do something to correct them. Go to where the people are, maybe wear less formal clothes. Help people with less power than you get the skills, networks and confidence they need to participate.

Chapter 7: Do good

Another world is not only possible,
she is on her way. On a quiet day,
I can hear her breathing.

The old politics is creaking on rough seas; its hull, so solid for so long, is splitting into fragments and tumbling in slow motion to the ocean floor. New political animals are emerging through the cracks in the old, broken systems. They are rising in bubbles to the surface – many, many tiny bubbles filled with the oxygen of new life. Around the world they are joining up – they are connecting, creating networks and using technology to participate and build movements. As we come together, we build our resilience in our own physical and mental health, in our relationships, and in our communities and our systems. When one part breaks, we will not fall down.

Writer and activist Arundhati Roy also wrote about the global pandemic as 'a portal, a gateway between one world and the next'. Right now we have a choice – we can cling with dear life to what's gone before, scrambling backwards to some sort of normal. Or we can step boldly forward towards what we can't yet see, making it up as we go. So imagine yourself at that gateway. Empty your bag of fear, cynicism and apathy, take a deep breath, step into your power as a new political animal and do good in your world.

Do good | 137

Everyone's a leader

I live in a beautiful city at the edge of the Southern Ocean, embraced by a mountain that curves around its south-western edge. The name given to the mountain by our First Nations people is *kunanyi*, and it's like it holds us all in and gives us the freedom to explore without falling off the edge. That's what leadership is like for new political animals. It spreads out its arms and holds the space for others to thrive.

We've relied on the heroic leader story for a long time now, holding out hope for that one individual, that perfect sum of humanity, who will swoop in and pluck us from disaster.

We've relied on the heroic leader story for a long time now, holding out hope for that one individual, that perfect sum of humanity, who will swoop in and pluck us from disaster. Well it's time to move on to something both ancient and new. That kind of just-in-time heroism is not sustainable in our complex, fast-paced world; in fact it has never been sustainable. We need to shift our view – instead of looking up for the leader who will give us the answer, we need to look alongside. Leadership is not a position; it's a practice and everyone can do it.

The practice of leadership requires you to work on yourself as you step out to share power with others. Let's go back to Chapter 3 where we talked about getting your three centres of intelligence in balance: your head, heart and body. Now we bring them together to show the three leadership qualities you need to cultivate as a new political animal (adapted here from the Presencing Institute's Theory U).

Curiosity: From your head centre, cultivate an open mind. Be curious so that you see problems as invitations; ask questions of yourself and others without judgment. You will notice you are out of balance when you hear yourself being judgmental.

Compassion: From your heart centre, cultivate an open heart. Work on your compassion so that you understand deeply where others are coming from, their situation and their potential. You will notice you are out of balance when you hear yourself being cynical.

Courage: From your body centre, cultivate an open will. Find the courage to step up and act in accordance with your values – to feel the fear and do it anyway. You will notice you are out of balance when you feel afraid to step out.

There are examples in all sorts of places of emotionally intelligent leaders shifting the power balance. During lockdown a local school ran a student wellbeing survey. The results came back and the principal noticed some consistent themes. One was that the students said they liked home schooling because they could be warm and comfortable. He was curious, so he asked some of the students what that was about. The answer surprised him. They said the school uniform left them feeling cold and they couldn't concentrate. He asked them what they wanted to do to fix it and they said they wanted to be able to wear hoodies. Hooded sweatshirts weren't part of the uniform and had been banned by the previous leadership of the school.

The principal gave the students permission to solve the problem in their own way. So they found some designs, consulted fellow students and the broader school community, and hoodies were available to purchase within a month. The principal created the space so that the students could lead, and this was possible because of his high level of emotional intelligence. He demonstrated curiosity and compassion, he was courageous enough to challenge an accepted truth of the school, and he had the ability to change it because of his position of power.

There are three key ingredients to making a change like this: awareness (deep understanding of the issues) **+ the courage to act** (challenge accepted truths) **+ the ability to act** (position of power).

With only the courage and ability to act, you may find yourself rushing to action without understanding what's really going on. With only the awareness of the problem and no courage or ability to act, you can become disillusioned and cynical. This is what happens on complex challenges like climate change. Survey after survey shows high levels of public awareness and concern about the crisis. Individuals around their kitchen tables are making decisions about the small steps they can take every day to make a difference for the planet. But the big decisions need to happen around the cabinet table, in parliaments and in boardrooms. Ninety-nine-point-nine-nine per cent of us aren't at those tables. We are concerned, we can see what's going on, but for real change to happen we need to engage in the strategies outlined in this book and lead in new ways.

Do things differently

'Doing things differently' isn't something you do occasionally at a workshop, it's something you need to cultivate every day, as new habits of thought and practices.

Einstein was a pretty smart guy, but not even he could have imagined the world we live in now. One of the very cool things he said was that we are not going to fix our problems with the same thinking that created them. Right now we're upending our thinking on lots of things and it can be scary. As you step out into the thick undergrowth you can feel unsafe – you're not sure what's ahead. But the more often you tread there, the clearer the path will become, paving the way for others to follow. 'Doing things differently' isn't something you do occasionally at a workshop, it's something you need to cultivate every day, as new habits of thought and practices.

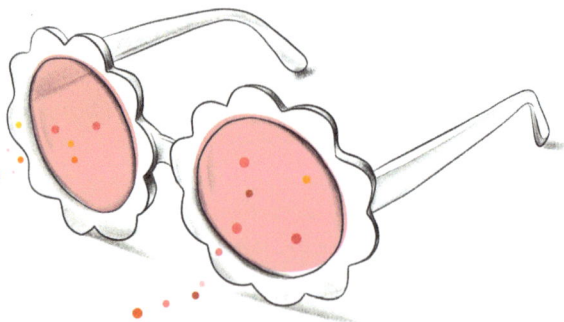

Take on the fresh eyes of a child and get in the habit of asking, 'Is there a better way?'

Think about how a child sees the world. So much is new all the time. The colours, the shadows and light. The ladybug on the leaf and the elephant shape in the clouds. Children have a beautiful naiveté that is somehow not a cool quality for an adult. Instead we slide towards cynicism – we've seen it all before. You know those people who are so jaded they drain the energy in the room? I once worked on a floor with two managers who had been there so long the sarcasm dripped daily from their mouths and turned the whole place toxic.

Political animals need to notice when this happens and keep it in check because it's infectious and inhibits creative problem-solving. Instead, find ways to create an environment for new ideas, stay open to what's possible and keep quiet on the reality check until later. Take on the fresh eyes of a child and get in the habit of asking, 'Is there a better way?'

Doing things differently is often about joining dots that haven't been joined before. In one community there were two needs: young people needed to get their driving hours up so they could get their licence, and older, immobile people needed to eat fresh food. The local community house started a program where learner drivers delivered food packages from the community garden to older people in the community. Two problems solved *and* trust being built across generations. Genius.

Because of our fear of failure we tend to hold onto our ideas until they're perfect before we put them out in the world.

As Thomas Edison famously said, 'I have not failed. I've just found 10,000 ways that didn't work'. So put your idea out there before it's perfect and see what happens.

Political animals need to redefine failure as invitations to learn. As Thomas Edison famously said, 'I have not failed. I've just found 10,000 ways that didn't work'. So put your idea out there before it's perfect and see what happens.

A few years ago, as a political adviser I was involved in an experiment in the way politicians listen to the people. We held the first in a series of community forums in a small suburban hall in my home state and used a different format. We dropped the traditional question-and-answer model, where the audience sits in rows asking questions of government ministers who are perched on a stage at the front. Instead, the ministers took seats at round tables with the local residents who had chosen to come along. Ministers were briefed on what to wear (no ties) and what to say (not much – the point was to listen). The sessions were run by highly skilled facilitators and all the politicians had to do was hold the space to let the conversation take its course.

At that first forum something remarkable happened. Sparks of connection lit up across the room like a plasma ball. A local resident raised concerns about graffiti. A local councillor responded, telling him about a program the council was looking at, and promised to chat more to him about it in the break. A community worker wanted more activities for young people so they could feel good about themselves. A minister said he'd put them in touch with people who ran a football program for kids and parents. A school principal talked about stigma and the need for positive stories to build confidence and pride. The people in the room who knew the editor of the local newspaper promised to have a word. And the positive stories kept coming. People stayed talking to each other over cups of tea and sandwiches long after the government ministers had left.

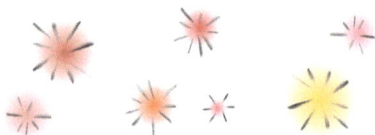

As the final task before the session wrapped up, the facilitators asked one of the ministers to reflect on what he had heard. He'd been briefed – he knew this was his role. But he couldn't quite manage it. Rather than talk about what he'd heard people say, he presented a neat list of issues, an outline of what the government was doing on some things and the party's position on what could be done about other things. That's okay; he's not to blame. The people in the room may not even have noticed. After all, it's what politicians do – they fix things. They have answers. They are experts. They have the power.

We must, now more than ever, create those spaces where sparks of connection can happen.

Imagine new political animals telling a different story. One where the government minister at the end of the morning's conversation acknowledged every person in that room and listed one thing he had heard each of them say. Imagine how the woman who talked about the young people would have felt if the politician had said to her, 'I heard that you really care about young people in your community and you want to make their lives better. I'd like to help you do that'. She would have felt respected, and valued, and heard.

Something else happens in this scenario. There's a shift in power.

Something else happens in this scenario. There's a shift in power. Instead of power being held tightly to the chest of the politician, it is set free to ripple out among the people. Instead of the government riding in on its white horse to fix a problem they don't fully understand, they hold the space so the people can fix it themselves

We must, now more than ever, create those spaces where sparks of connection can happen, where new ideas can build on each other into towers of possibility that carry us through the portal to whatever comes next.

Tell your story

It's human nature to respond to stories. When you share your story of change you challenge people's perceptions and inspire them. Maybe you are one of those people who hate talking about yourself, so it may be easier for you if you hold this thought: it's not about you. When you share your story you motivate others to take action, to participate in activities and to influence other people. I'm not saying you need to grab the microphone at the front of the rally; you just need to know that your story can be powerful when it's told to people who are ready to listen, no matter how quietly or how publicly.

There are many ways you can structure your story. The best one I've found is from Marshall Ganz, Senior Lecturer in Leadership, Organizing and Civil Society at the Kennedy School of Government, Harvard University. He promotes the simple structure, 'self, us, now' as part of his public narrative teaching. Watch speeches by any contemporary US Democrat politician and you will see this format come to life.

Start your story with 'self': we all have a story, and what's unique is our journey of learning to be a whole

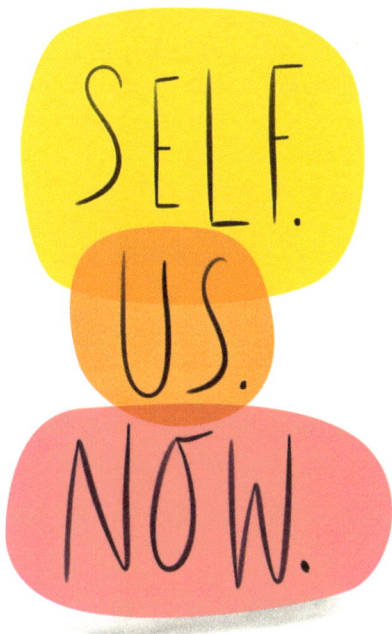

SELF. US. NOW.

human being. Your listeners will connect with you when you talk about your journey and the barriers and challenges you've had to overcome. Then move on to 'us': We all have experiences and values that we share as a community. Share why your story is common to everyone, how we are connected by our experience of both the pain and the hopefulness of the world. Finish with 'now': The story of 'now' is the tension between the world as we want it to be and the world as it is. This creates the urgency that drives us forward. It forces us to consider a choice. What do we do about that? Ganz says we're called to answer this question in a spirit of hope. Our goal is to meet this challenge, to seize this hope, and turn it into concrete action.

Think about a powerful personal story you've heard, perhaps like that of Grace Tame, advocate for survivors of sexual assault and 2021 Australian of the Year. What do you connect to in her story? What values do you relate to? What shift, no matter how tiny, has occurred in your thinking as a result of hearing this story? You too can inspire others with your story, and by sharing it you can challenge accepted truths and change the public narrative.

Play the long game

The sort of change we're talking about is not easy, especially when power is being wrested from the arms of people who have held it for a long time.

While political animals must always step forward in the spirit of hope, I don't want to leave you with the impression that it's all *kumbaya*, and that if we hold hands round the campfire everything will be okay. The sort of change we're talking about is not easy, especially when power is being wrested from the arms of people who have held it for a long time.

They will fight like hell to keep things the way they are. So for now new political animals need to keep one foot in the brutal pragmatism of the old politics as they reach out to shape the new. Shaping a better world, and changing the way we do politics, requires you to play the long game.

While you may be impatient to fix things and the solutions may be obvious to you, now may not be the right time. I've met so many idealists who have worn themselves out trying to get change and being blocked at every turn. Like Aden, the community development officer in a local council who is on a mission to expand the focus of elected members beyond the traditional 'roads, rates and rubbish' to the health and wellbeing of ratepayers. He has his moments where he wants to give up, but then he'll have a small win, like funding for a pilot program for homeless youth. The many losses are easier to deal with if you have your eye on the long game.

Our political animal, Chris, is a master of playing the long game. As an advocate for social change she has had to do a lot of compromising, negotiating and letting go in order to achieve positive outcomes for her constituents. There have been many occasions when she was on the brink of walking away, but she bit her tongue and held on. Playing the long game required her to let go of her own idea of what the best solutions are, and to stop listening to her own ego, which was telling her she was right.

There is a lot of change that can happen on the way to your goal. You can build alliances that last a lifetime.

To be an influencer for long-term outcomes Chris takes a non-adversarial, low-key tone, so she isn't judged, labelled and marginalised. Having high emotional intelligence, Chris checks herself before voicing her opinion to make sure she advances the cause of people she represents, rather than serving her own ego and pride. She believes that right will win out when you care about the people who benefit from the change. It is the job of political animals to keep holding the space and be prepared to wait for a time to pitch into a different room.

There is a lot of change that can happen on the way to your goal. You can build alliances that last a lifetime. You can help people on your team gain the confidence to lead. You can inspire others to join your cause. But you may waste your energy if you try to persuade people who hold tightly to their views. Instead you need to create the conditions for change. This is what happened during the marriage equality debate in Australia, and it's what is happening right now in conversations in many countries about ideas like universal basic income. The focus of the effort is to turn an idea from inconceivable into inevitable, so that those who resist the change can no longer hold back the tide.

Final lessons

When you're playing the long game there are some important final lessons to remember:

Do your strategy: Set yourself a clear objective – where you want to be and when – and write it down. Deeply understand the problem you are trying to solve and ask yourself why it hasn't been solved before. Work out who your people are – the ones impacted by the change and your allies. What resources do they bring? Then choose the best tactics from your kit, such as direct conversations with decision-makers, seeding ideas with influencers, and using public pressure.

Choose your battles: Political animals know when to hold and when to fold (and when to walk away and when to run). Now may not be the right time for this battle; you might have to pass on a small fight in pursuit of a bigger change. You may have given it all you can and you're getting nowhere. In fact, you could be going backwards if you are damaging relationships or your reputation is at risk. So put it in the bottom drawer for now. There will be another time in the future.

Throw rocks sometimes: It's nice to be all very rational and reasonable, but sometimes you've just had enough and you explode. This is what former Australian Prime Minister Julia Gillard did in what's now known as her 'misogyny speech'. Spontaneous or not, it's an effective tactic, captured well by Don Watson in *Recollections of a Bleeding Heart*, about another former Prime Minister, Paul Keating: 'Sometimes ... you have to pick up a bloody big rock and drop it in the pond. One minute all the frogs are sitting around on their old familiar lily pads, singing the same old songs, thinking the same old thoughts – everything in its proper place in what seems the natural order. And then there's this bloody great tidal wave and when they look around the next time the world has changed'.

Don't burn your bridges: As we know, relationships are key. You have to make a judgment about whether what you're fighting for is worth destroying long-term relationships. You may have a lot to say and you want to be your authentic self, but it may not be smart to offload right now. Learn how to keep quiet.

Take the good: It was Voltaire who said, 'The best is the enemy of the good'. You may have a crystal-clear view of the change you want to create and feel virtuous for holding true to your principles and your values. But there's not much point going to your grave feeling great about yourself when you could actually have made a small change that benefits other people. It's better to achieve something than nothing at all. So be prepared to let go of some of the things you hold close. Ask yourself, 'Can I live with it? Am I going to die in a ditch over it?'

Don't be precious: This can be hard. If you let yourself be your ideas, then your ego can get in the way. To be really Buddhist about it you need to set the idea free, and if your boss takes it on as their own then good luck to them. The main thing is that it gets done. Hand it over and be proud. (And put your strategy in place to make sure it's you who is the boss next time.)

Be discreet: Hold onto your integrity. Old political animals thrive on gossip. It is toxic. When someone complains to you about someone else you know instinctively that they are likely to do the same about you. Don't bitch about people – offload with your partner or your mum, not with your colleagues. When you are discreet, people are more likely to tell you what's going on.

Don't air your dirty laundry in public: Groups that push for progressive social change have a tendency to fight with each other in public. Political animals need to be more like the Hong Kong democracy protesters who made a pact not to criticise each other in public. The 'braves' and the 'peacefuls' had very different views on tactics, but they put forward a united front so they couldn't be picked off by the government.

Get a seat at the table: It's easy to criticise when you're not the one who's responsible for the solution. Former Australian Prime Minister Gough Whitlam famously said about the Left members of his own party, who were protesting his decisions, 'Certainly, the impotent are pure'. So get yourself into a position where you make the decision.

What does the future look like?

The crisis that took hold of 2020 and shook it like a snow globe has in fact placed in our hands a profound opportunity for transformation. We have the chance to shape this moment, just as our forebears did last century when they seized global cooperation out of the devastation of war and made the United Nations and the Universal Declaration of Human Rights. Now, in among the visible reclamations of power by citizens protesting in streets around the world, are the quiet shifts at home, in workplaces and in neighbourhoods. You may be experiencing these shifts in thinking and behaviour yourself, and you may have friends and family members who are now reflecting and making different decisions about what's important to them.

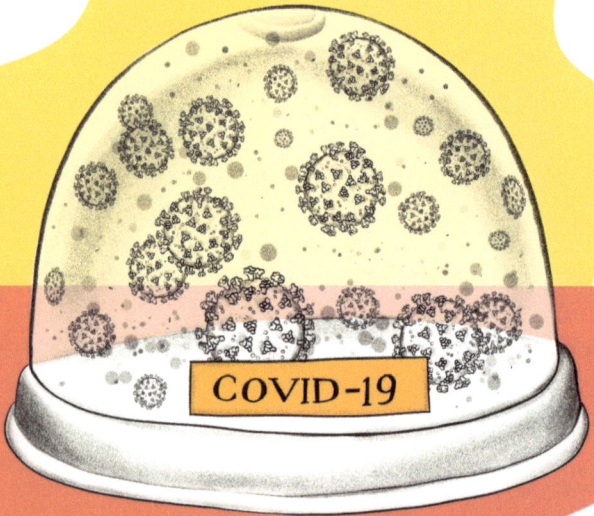

Accepted truths about the way we work are being challenged, with decisions being made that bring greater balance to the lives of employees, to the point where there are declarations that the nine-to-five work day is dead. Accepted truths about the way we are governed are being challenged, with people organising better ways to participate in the decisions that affect them. People are finding the courage to challenge the accepted truths about the unequal treatment of members of our society through social movements.

Bureaucrats and policy-makers are embracing co-design methods and are putting the voices of marginalised communities at the centre of decisions. Attention is turning to sustainable solutions through the knowledge systems of Indigenous people as we grapple with the climate crisis and species extinction. Following us is emerging a tenacious, resourceful and collaborative generation that will keep pushing for positive change for the sustainability of people and our planet.

There are signs that we are creating a world where power is held in the hands of the many.

We don't yet know where this is all heading, and strong forces are tightening their grip on power. But there are signs that we are creating a world where power is held in the hands of the many. And this is being made real in the decisions people are making every day. You don't need to lead a rally, or start a movement (yet), you just need to undertake small acts of personal courage. You need to gently and powerfully challenge accepted truths. You need to speak from the heart and tell a story of hope. You need to step out and use your power to lift up others to do some good in your world.

We are the many, and we need to act now. This is our moment. When we come together as new political animals to act for the benefit of others, to create a better world, we are more powerful than we could ever know.

PRACTICE TIPS

We are in a profound period of disruption and transformation. It's like a tug-of-war with the old war horses terrified as they feel their grip on power loosening. People are waking up to all the poor decisions that we've let slide for years and they are stepping into their own power, propelled by the need to live a good life on a planet that can sustain life. There is a lot that the old politics can teach us about being pragmatic and playing the long game. Political animals must now take those lessons and forge a new path as politically intelligent, emotionally intelligent leaders who are using their power to make better decisions every day, wherever they are.

Leadership

Take time to reflect on who you are as a leader and who you could be. Ask yourself:

In leading change, what resources do I have (in myself and my world)?

What fears do I have? What stops me speaking out when something needs to be said?

What needs to change? What can I do differently?

How will I help others while I am becoming my best self?

Over to you

When you wake up tomorrow...

What will you pay attention to?

What one thing will you change about yourself?

Which friend will you ask to help you?

Where will you target your effort?

How will you organise your people?

What next step will you take to do good in your world?

References

Introduction

Aristotle, *Politics* (B Jowett translation) (Dover Thrift Editions), 2000

Hannah Arendt (Hannah Arendt Centre for Politics and Humanities): www.hac.bard.edu

Chapter 1

Joan Kirner and Moira Rayner, *The Women's Power Handbook* (Penguin Books Australia), 1999

Jeremy Heimans, and Henry Timms, *New Power* (Anchor Books), 2018

Chapter 2

Oxfam, 'World's billionaires have more wealth than 4.6 billion people', published 20 January 2020

ABC News, 'Bronwyn Bishop spends $5000 on 80km charter helicopter flight from Melbourne to Geelong', posted 15 July 2015, 3.30pm (updated 7.43pm)

Commonwealth of Australia, 'An Independent Parliamentary Entitlements System Review', February 2016

Department of Jobs and Small Business, 'I Want to Work: Employment Services 2020 Report', December 2018

Chapter 3

Daniel Goleman, *Working with Emotional Intelligence* (Bloomsbury Publishing), 1998

Malcolm Turnbull interview with Leigh Sales, *7.30* (ABC TV), 21 September 2015

Global Leadership Foundation: www.globalleadershipfoundation.com

Malcolm Lazenby and Gayle Hardie, *Working with Emotional Health and the Enneagram* (Monterey Press), 2019

Chapter 4

Greta Thunberg, speech to the World Economic Forum, 25 January 2019

Cathy Burke, *Unlikely Leaders* (Cathy Burke), 2015

Presencing Institute (Theory U): www.presencing.org/aboutus/theory-u

Don Watson, *Recollections of a Bleeding Heart: A portrait of Paul Keating PM* (Random House Australia), 2002

Otto Scharmer: www.ottoscharmer.com

Chapter 5

Sun Tzu, *The Art of War* (Penguin Classics), 2008

Chapter 6

Stacey Abrams (Fair Fight): www. fairfight.com

Compass UK (40° Change): www.compassonline.org.uk

Chapter 7

Arundhati Roy, 'The pandemic is a portal', Financial Times, 4 April 2020

Marshall Ganz: www.marshallganz.com

Grace Tame (The Grace Tame Foundation): www.thegracetamefoundation.org.au

Julia Gillard, the 'Misogyny Speech', Australian Parliament, 9 October 2012

Gough Whitlam, speech to the annual conference of the Victorian Branch of the Australian Labor Party, 9 June 1967

Acknowledgments

Thank you to the people who have contributed to this book through their wisdom, advice, support and encouragement: Yvette Cehtel, Kym Goodes, Kate Gross, Melanie Lambert, Lisa Singh, Lisa Schimanski, and the fledgling political animals who have shared their stories. Thank you to clever editors and advisers, David Brewster and Heather Kelly, and talented designer and illustrator Cathy McAuliffe. And thank you with love to my family who have always given my words a safe place to land.

www.ingramcontent.com/pod-product-compliance
Lightning Source LLC
Chambersburg PA
CBHW040932050426
42334CB00047B/112